FUNDAMENTAL SPEECHES
From Five Decades

JOSEPH RATZINGER
POPE BENEDICT XVI

FUNDAMENTAL SPEECHES
From Five Decades

Edited by Florian Schuller

Translated by Michael J. Miller,
J. R. Foster, and Adrian Walker

IGNATIUS PRESS   SAN FRANCISCO

Original German edition:
Grundsatz-Reden aus fünf Jahrzehnten
© 2005 by Verlag Pustet, Regensburg

Photograph of Pope Benedict XVI
© Stefano Spaziani

Cover design by Roxanne Mei Lum

ISBN 978-1-58617-303-6
Library of Congress Control Number 2011940708
Printed in the United States of America ∞

CONTENTS

TRIBUTES

FOREWORD

by Florian Schuller

"We must ask how the Academy, as a place for interpretation, is to be understood in the contrasting light of contemplation and action." This was the question posed by
Joseph Cardinal Ratzinger, who at that time had been working in Rome for seven months, on the occasion of the meeting celebrating the twenty-fifth anniversary of the Catholic
Academy of Bavaria.

For more than forty years, Joseph Ratzinger again and
again gave an answer in our House, whose task according to its constitutions is "to clarify and promote relations between the Church and the world". In keeping with
this mission statement, the directors of the Academy—Karl
Forster, Franz Henrich, and in 2004 the undersigned as well
—invited him to reflect on a wide range of topics.

Joseph Ratzinger lectured at our meetings seventeen times
in all, as a professor from Bonn, Münster, Tübingen, and
Regensburg, as Archbishop of Munich and Freising, and as
Prefect of the Congregation for the Doctrine of the Faith.
Eleven of these lectures were published in a form that he
authorized. When we read through them again, we were surprised by their lasting relevance and are therefore presenting them as an anthology—as fundamental speeches that dis-
play the breadth and core of the theological thought of Pope
Benedict XVI.

Certainly, an inquiry like the one from the turbulent [late

7

1960s and early] 1970s would not necessarily be formulated today as: "Why I Am Still in the Church". That the problems expressed in the title have meanwhile intensified drastically, however, needs no proof. Thus there is not only a special charm in studying a document by a theologian and bishop who has since been elected pope that states the reasons why he "still" is in the Church, but at the same time the reader gets a concise commentary on what it means to be a believer in the Church, an explanation that goes much deeper than the usual discussion of arguments pro and con.

The text that has made the most profound impression on the intellectual consciousness of discerning contemporaries is probably the statement that Cardinal Ratzinger made in his dialogue with Jürgen Habermas. At the invitation of the Academy, the representative par excellence of secular rational thought met in January 2004 for the first time with the most important representative of Catholic faith-based reflection. In acknowledgment of the intellectual vigor of the new pope, this encounter was regularly recalled on editorial pages and interpreted as a signal of new alliances in dialogue despite ongoing differences about basic principles.

The reader will find these fundamental speeches arranged, not chronologically, but thematically, starting with a paper that the newly appointed cardinal presented in October 1977 at a conference in Rome on the topic of "The Nature and Commission of the Petrine Ministry". The interpretation set forth in it not only can help us to understand in general how Pope Benedict XVI views the Petrine office in its ministry of establishing unity, which has now been entrusted to him, but also explains the surprising emphasis in his homily after his election, when he called the ecumenical endeavor one of the primary challenges that must be addressed.

Next come three texts on central tenets of the Creed and

two theological reflections on the Church. The task of the Christian faith in the world likewise plays an important role in three papers, a fact due to an intellectual development that was formulated with explosive force and logical consistency in Joseph Ratzinger's lecture on "Europe, a Heritage with Obligations for Christians", which after more than twenty-five years still has political relevance as well.

The conclusion consists of two tributes. The Bavarian Prime Minister Alfons Goppel and Romano Guardini are precisely delineated as individual personalities, and their accomplishments are systematically evaluated.

One sentence in this book can serve as a summary of the abiding core of Joseph Ratzinger's convictions, one that will leave its mark on his pontificate and is not only his message to us but the message of Christianity in general: "The hope of Christianity, the prospect of faith is ultimately based quite simply on the fact that it tells the truth." The interpretations presented here help us to speak the truth of Christianity in the dialogue of hearts and minds; they are meant to spur us to action and to open the way to that contemplation from which they were born.

With Pope John Paul II at the meeting of the Pope with artists and journalists in the Hercules Hall of the Royal Residence in Munich, which was planned and organized by the Catholic Academy in Bavaria; November 19, 1980 (Photograph: Academy Archive/Felici).

The Petrine Ministry

In the year when Professor Joseph Ratzinger was appointed Archbishop of Munich and Freising and raised to the rank of cardinal, the Catholic Academy in Bavaria conducted an academic symposium in Rome from October 11–14, 1977, which was dedicated to the theme of "Service to Unity: On the Nature and Commission of the Petrine Ministry". The occasion was the eightieth birthday of Pope Paul VI and the presence of the Bavarian bishops for their ad limina visit in Rome. The contribution by Joseph Cardinal Ratzinger reprinted here presented an outline of a martyrologically understood interpretation of the papal primacy from the ecumenical perspective and, at the same time, an outlook on the future situation of Christianity that emphasized the unifying function of the papacy as a permanent commission. The lecture served as the conclusion of an event that dealt with the topic from the perspectives of exegesis, Church history, systematic theology, and ecumenism. Among the internationally renowned lecturers were also Professor Alberigo (Bologna), Professor Jean-Jacques von Allmen (Neuburg), Professor Walter Kasper (Tübingen), Professor Franz Mußner (Regensburg), and Professor Wilhelm de Vries, S.J. (Rome).

THE PRIMACY OF THE POPE AND THE UNITY OF THE PEOPLE OF GOD

I. The Spiritual Basis for Primacy and Collegiality

The papacy is not one of the popular topics of the post-conciliar period. To a certain extent it was something self-evident as long as the monarchy corresponded to it in the political realm. Ever since the monarchic idea became extinct in practice and was replaced by the democratic idea, the doctrine of papal primacy has lacked a point of reference within the scope of our common intellectual assumptions. So it is certainly no accident that the First Vatican Council was dominated by the idea of primacy, while the Second was characterized mainly by the struggle over the concept of collegiality.[1] Of course, we should immediately add that, in adopting the idea of collegiality (along with other initiatives from contemporary life), the Second Vatican Council sought to describe it in such a way that the idea of primacy was contained within it. Today, now that we have gained a little experience with collegiality, its value and also its limitations, it looks as though we have to start again precisely at this place in order to understand better how these seemingly

Translated by Michael J. Miller.

[1] H. J. Pottmeyer sheds light on the intellectual-historical context in which the First Vatican Council should be viewed; see his book *Unfehlbarkeit und Souveränität: Die päpstliche Unfehlbarkeit im System der ultramontanen Ekklesiologie des 19. Jahrhunderts*, Tübinger theologische Studien 5 (Mainz, 1975).

contrary traditions belong together and thus to preserve the richness of the Christian reality.

1. Collegiality as the expression of the "we" structure of the faith

In connection with the conciliar debate, theology had tried, in due course, to understand collegiality as something more than a merely structural or functional feature: as a fundamental law that extends into the innermost essential foundations of Christianity and that therefore appears in various ways on the individual levels of Christianity as it is actually put into practice. It was possible to demonstrate that the "we" structure was part of Christianity in the first place.[2] The believer, as such, never stands alone: to become a believer means to emerge from isolation into the "we" of the children of God; the act of turning to the God revealed in Christ is always a turning also to those who have already been called. The theological act as such is always an ecclesial act, which also has a characteristically social structure.[3] Hence initiation into Christianity has always been socialization into the commu-

[2] I tried in 1965 to set forth the spiritual background for collegiality in the "we" structure of Christianity in my essay for *Concilium* (English ed., vol. 1, no. 1 [January 1965]: 20–34), "The Pastoral Implications of Episcopal Collegiality", which was reprinted in the original German in J. Ratzinger, *Das neue Volk Gottes* (Düsseldorf, 1969), 201–24. A thoroughgoing treatment of the problem is the important book by H. Mühlen, *Una mystica persona: Die Kirche als Mysterium der Identität des Heiligen Geistes in Christus und der Kirche: Eine Person in vielen Personen*, 3rd ed. (Paderborn, 1968).

[3] Henri de Lubac explained this strikingly in his book *Catholicisme*, which first appeared in 1938 [translated by Lancelot C. Sheppard and Elizabeth Englund as *Catholicism: Christ and the Common Destiny of Man* (San Francisco: Ignatius Press, 1988)]. See also the dissertation written by H. Schnackers as a doctoral student at the University of Regens-

nity of believers as well, becoming "we", which surpasses the mere "I".[4] Accordingly, Jesus called his disciples to form the Twelve, which recalls the number of tribes in the ancient People of God, an essential feature of which, in turn, is the fact that God creates a communal history and deals with his people as a people.[5] On the other hand, the most profound reason for this "we" character of Christianity proved to be the fact that God himself is a "we": the God professed in the Christian Creed is not a lonely self-reflection of thought or an absolutely and indivisibly self-contained "I", but rather he is unity in the trinitarian relation of I-you-we, so that being "we", as the fundamental form of divinity, precedes all worldly instances of "we", and the image and likeness of God necessarily refers to such being "we" from the very beginning.[6]

---

burg: *Kirche als Sakrament und Mutter* (1976). In Germany, this same approach was developed particularly in the studies of H. Poschmann on the theology of the sacrament of reconciliation, especially *Poenitentia secunda* (Bonn, 1940); it was impressively continued by K. Rahner—for example, in his essay "Forgotten Truths concerning the Sacrament of Penance", *Theological Investigations* (London and Baltimore, 1963), 2:135–74.

[4] Initiation as ecclesial socialization is very strongly emphasized in the section entitled "Eingliederung in die Kirche", in the book *Pastorale: Handreichung für den pastoralen Dienst*, by G. Biemer, J. Müller, and R. Zerfaß (Mainz, 1972).

[5] On the significance of the Twelve, see, for example, R. Schnackenburg, *The Church in the New Testament*, trans. W. J. O'Hara (London, 1965), 22–35; on the conciliar application of the theme, see G. Philips, *L'Église et son mystère au IIe concile du Vatican*, vol. 1 (Paris, 1967), 277–90 and 230–45.

[6] Cf. Henri de Lubac, *The Christian Faith: An Essay on the Structure of the Apostles' Creed*, trans. Richard Arnandez (San Francisco: Ignatius Press, 1986), 55–84; Joseph Ratzinger, *Introduction to Christianity*, trans. J. R. Foster, rev. ed. (San Francisco: Ignatius Press, 2004); H. Mühlen, *Una mystica persona*.

In this connection, a treatise by E. Peterson on "Mono-theism as a Political Problem", which had been largely for-gotten, again became a matter of current interest. In it, Pe-terson tried to show that Arianism was a political theology favored by the emperors because it ensured a divine anal-ogy to the political monarchy, whereas the triumph of the trinitarian faith exploded political theology and removed the theological justification for political monarchy.[7] Peterson in-terrupted his presentation at this point; now it was taken up again and continued with a new analogous thought, the ba-sic thrust of which was: God's "we" must be the model for the action of the Church as a "we". This general approach, which can be interpreted in various ways, was in a few cases taken so far as to claim that, accordingly, the exercise of the primacy by a single man, the pope in Rome, actually fol-lows an Arian model. In keeping with the three Persons in God, the argument went, the Church must also be led by a college of three, and the members of this triumvirate, acting together, would be the pope. There was no lack of ingenious speculations that (alluding, for instance, to Soloviev's story about the Antichrist) discovered that in this way a Roman Catholic, an Orthodox, and a Protestant together could form the papal troika. Thus it appeared that the ultimate formula for ecumenism had been found, derived immediately from theo-logy (from the concept of God), that they had discov-ered a way to square the circle, whereby the papacy, the chief stumbling block for non-Catholic Christianity, would have to become the definitive vehicle for bringing about the unity of all Christians.[8]

---

[7] Reprinted in E. Peterson, *Theologische Traktate* (Munich, 1951), 45–147; first published in 1935. The set of historical problems involved in Peterson's thesis becomes evident in A. Grillmeier, *Mit ihm und in ihm: Christologische Forschungen und Perspektiven* (Freiburg, 1975), 386–419.

[8] Such things could occasionally be heard in spoken remarks that may

2. *The interior basis for the primacy: Faith as responsible personal witness*

Is this, then—the reconciliation of collegiality and primacy —the answer to the question posed by our subject: the primacy of the pope and the unity of the People of God? Although we need not conclude that such reflections are *entirely* sterile and useless, it is plain that they are a distortion of trinitarian doctrine and an intolerably oversimplified fusion of Creed and Church polity. What is needed is a more profound approach. It seems to me that it is important, first of all, to reestablish a clearer connection between the theology of communion, which had developed from the idea of collegiality, and a theology of personality, which is no less important in interpreting the biblical facts. Not only does the communal character of the history created by God belong to the structure of the Bible, but also and equally personal responsibility. The "we" does not dissolve the "I" and "you", but rather it confirms and intensifies them so as to make them almost definitive. This is evident already in the importance that a name has in the Old Testament—for God and for men. One could even say that in the Bible "name" takes the place of what philosophical reflection would eventually designate by the word "person".[9] Corresponding to God, who has a name, that is, who can address others and be addressed, is man, who is called by name in the history

have roughly paraphrased discussions by H. Mühlen, especially in his book *Entsakralisierung* (Paderborn, 1971), 228ff., 240ff., 376–96, 401–40. Although Mühlen's own arguments are striking and advance scholarship, it seems to me they are not free of the danger of a new analogous way of thinking that exaggerates the applicability of the trinitarian doctrine to ecclesiology.

[9] Cf. J. Ratzinger, *The God of Jesus Christ: Meditations on the Triune God*, trans. Brian McNeil (San Francisco: Ignatius Press, 2008), 15–25.

of revelation and is held personally responsible.[10] This principle is further intensified in the New Testament and attains its fullest, deepest meaning through the fact that now
the People of God is generated, not by birth, but rather by
a call and a response. Therefore it is no longer a collective
consignee as before, when the whole people functioned as a
sort of corporate individual vis-à-vis world history, in collective punishment, in collective liability, penance, and pardon.
The "new people" is characterized also by a new structure
of personal responsibility, which is manifest in the personal-
izing of the cultic event: from now on everyone is named by
name in penance and, as a consequence of the personal baptism that he received as this particular person, is also called
by name to do personal penance, for which the general "we
have sinned" can no longer be an adequate substitute.[11] Another consequence of this structure is, for example, the fact
that the liturgy does not simply speak about the Church
in general but presents her by name in the Canon of the
Mass: with the names of the saints and the names of those
who bear the responsibility for unity. From this perspective,
incidentally, it seemed to me questionable that in the first
German version of the liturgical Lectionary the names were
omitted (probably for fear of making historically inaccurate
attributions), and Saint Paul's Letter to the Romans, for instance, was no longer presented with the Apostle's name and
authority; rather, it was presented as an anonymous text of
uncertain provenance and with no one to vouch for it personally.[12]

[10] Cf. the significance of the genealogies in the structure of biblical
history.

[11] This is incisively elaborated in H. U. von Balthasar, "Umkehr im
Neuen Testament", *Internationale katholische Zeitschrift* 3 (1974): 481–91.

[12] Although the intention was to avoid the problem of the disputed
authorship of some texts, this was an example of mistaking the level and

It is in keeping with this personal structure, furthermore, that in the Church there has never been anonymous leadership of the Christian community. Paul writes in his own name as the one ultimately responsible for his congregations. But again and again he addresses by name those also who hold authority with him and under him; recall the lists of greetings in 1 Corinthians and the Letter to the Romans, or the comment in 1 Corinthians 4:17: "Therefore I sent you Timothy . . . , to remind you of my ways in Christ, as I teach them everywhere in every Church"; or the Letter to the Philippians, in which Paul (4:2) singles out Euodia and Syntyche and addresses his "true co-worker" in the second person singular. Along these same lines, lists of bishops were compiled already at the beginning of the second century (Hegesippus) so as to emphasize for the historical record the particular and personal responsibility of those witnesses to Jesus Christ.[13] This process is profoundly in keeping with the central structure of the New Testament faith: to *the one* witness, Jesus Christ, correspond *the many* witnesses who, precisely because they are witnesses, stand up for him by name. Martyrdom as a response to the Cross of Jesus Christ is nothing other than the ultimate confirmation of this principle of uncompromising particularity, of the named individual who is personally responsible.[14]

---

misunderstanding the liturgical message, which necessarily stands on the firm historical ground of the faith but must not be viewed as a forum in which to decide historical debates.

[13] The structural importance of these lists as reference points for the concept of tradition in the structure of Eusebius' *Ecclesiastical History* is demonstrated in a dissertation by V. Twomey on ecclesiology in the works of Eusebius and Athanasius.

[14] The essential meaning of martyrdom in the structure of the Christian act of faith is beautifully set forth by K. Bommes, *Weizen Gottes: Untersuchungen zur Theologie des Martyriums bei Ignatius von Antiochien* (Cologne

Witness implies particularity, but witness—as a response to the Cross and Resurrection—is the primordial and fundamental form of Christian discipleship in general. In addition, however, even this principle is anchored in the very belief in the triune God, for the Trinity becomes meaningful for us and recognizable in the first place through the fact that God himself, in his Son as man, became a witness to himself, and thus his personal nature took concrete form even unto the radical anthropomorphism of the "form of a servant", of "the likeness of men" (μορφὴ δούλου, ὁμοίωμα ἀνθρώπου: Phil 2:7).[15]

The Petrine theology of the New Testament is found along this line of reasoning, and therein it has its intrinsically necessary character. The "we" of the Church begins with the name of the one who in particular and as a person first uttered the profession of faith in Christ: "You are . . . the Son of the living God" (Mt 16:16). Curiously, the passage on the primacy is usually thought to begin with Matthew 16:17, whereas the early Church regarded verse 16 as the decisive verse for an understanding of the whole account: Peter becomes the Rock of the Church as the bearer of the *Credo*, of her faith in God, which is a concrete faith in Christ as the Son and by that very fact faith in the Father and, thus, a trinitarian faith, which only the Spirit of God can communicate.[16] The early Church viewed verses 17–19

---

and Bonn, 1976); see also E. Peterson, "Zeuge der Wahrheit", in *Theologische Traktate*, 165–224. The fact that martyrdom can find no place in Hans Küng's *On Being a Christian*, trans. Edward Quinn (London, 1977), 573–76 (see also the summary of the basic thesis, 601f.), is, from this perspective, quite telling.

[15] For an exegesis of this fundamental passage, see J. Gnilka, *Der Philipperbrief* (Freiburg, 1968), 111–47.

[16] Not to have noticed this is the weakness of the otherwise commendable study by J. Ludwig, *Die Primatworte Mt 16, 18.19 in der altkirchlichen*

as simply the explanation of verse 16: To recite the Creed is never man's own work, and thus the one who says in the obedience of the profession of faith what he cannot say on his own can also do and become what he could not do and become by his own resources. This perspective does not include the "either-or" that was first suggested in Augustine and has dominated the theological scene since the sixteenth century, when the alternative was formulated: Is Peter as a *person* the foundation of the Church, or is his *profession of faith* the foundation of the Church? The answer is: The profession of faith exists only as something for which someone is personally responsible, and hence the profession of faith is connected with the person. Conversely, the foundation is not a person regarded in a metaphysically neutral way, so to speak, but rather the person as the bearer of the profession of faith—one without the other would miss the significance of what is meant.

Leaving out many intermediate steps in the argument, we can say, then: The "we" unity of Christians, which God instituted in Christ through the Holy Spirit under the name of Jesus Christ and as a result of his witness, certified by his death and Resurrection, is in turn maintained by personal bearers of responsibility for this unity, and it is once again personified in Peter—in Peter, who receives a new name and is thus lifted up out of what is merely his own, yet precisely in a *name*, through which demands are made of him as a person with personal responsibility. In his new name,

---

Exegese, Neutestamentliche Abhandlungen, ed. M. Meinertz, vol. 19, no. 4 (Münster, 1954). This bars the way to an understanding of Leo the Great, but all the other Church Fathers, too, should be reexamined thoroughly in terms of an inquiry that is not so narrowly framed. Compare Stefan Horn's book *Petrou Kathedra: Der Bischof von Rom und die Synode von Ephesus und Chalcedon* (Paderborn: Verlag Bonifatius-Druckerei, 1982), which corrects the omissions in Ludwig's study.

which transcends the historical individual, Peter becomes the institution that goes through history (for the ability to continue and continuance are included in this new appellation), yet in such a way that this institution can exist only as a person and in particular and personal responsibility.

II. Retrospective Proof:
The Martyrological Structure of the Primacy

At this point a question arises that has become increasingly dramatic since the sixteenth century: Do not the demands that are made along with the name of Peter altogether exceed the dimensions of a human being? Can this extreme claim of the personality principle still be justified, both anthropologically and also from the basic perspective of the Bible? Or is it such that it befits Christ alone, and, consequently, applying it to a "Vicar of Christ" can only violate the principle of *solus Christus*? If so, then that would answer the single exegetical question, from the overall perspective, to the effect that any Petrine theology of the type just described would contradict the core statements of the New Testament and, consequently, should be called apostasy. It is true that any evaluation of individual exegetical findings depends on an overall perspective, and it follows that the decision, pro or con, cannot be made solely in the exegesis of a particular passage. Moreover, today, as F. Mußner has convincingly made clear, there is hardly any disputing, on the basis of the particular findings, the existence of a Petrine theology and a Petrine ministry that were meant to be lasting;[17] on the

[17] Cf. F. Mußner, "Petrusgestalt und Petrusdienst in der Sicht der späten Urkirche: Redaktionsgeschichtliche Überlegungen", in *Dienst an der Einheit*, ed. J. Ratzinger (Düsseldorf, 1978), 27–45.

other hand, the overall perspective of the New Testament seems to be all the more tellingly opposed to such a ministry. (Meanwhile the idea of a merely pastoral primacy, without juridical status, can be left out of consideration as factually irrelevant.)[18]

1. The witness structure of the primacy as the necessary consequence of the opposition of world and Church

I will attempt to give an answer to the question, thus framed, in connection with a historical controversy that, in my opinion, has retained its exemplary character and has led to the development of one of the most profound theologies of the primacy, in which the ecumenical dimension of the topic is preserved in a way hardly to be found anywhere else. I mean the debate that Reginald Cardinal Pole conducted with King Henry VIII, Cranmer, and Bishop Sampson with regard to the events in the Church of England concerning the primacy. We can see the real relevance of these questions for Pole from the fact that his life and homeland were at stake, on the one hand, and, on the other hand, that he was the favored candidate in the papal elections during the conclave of 1549–1550 and was thought for a moment to have been elected; finally, it should be added that in the final years of his life he was suspected of advocating a Lutheran doctrine of justification and of being a heretic himself.[19] Pole was

[18] This idea, which was proposed by Luther in the Leipzig Disputation, adopted by Melanchthon, and recently revived by Hans Küng, is still unrealistic: a responsibility that cannot be responsible is no responsibility at all.

[19] On this subject, see the dissertation by M. Trimpe, *Macht aus Gehorsam: Grundmotive der Theologie des päpstlichen Primats im Denken Reginald Poles (1500–1558)* (dissertation, University of Regensburg, 1972). The following discussion of Pole draws on this study. See also W. Schenk,

confronted with Sampson's thesis that the papacy as such
contradicted Christian humility and was from the outset
incompatible with it—substantially the very same opinion
that we described previously, in somewhat different words,
as the central theological objection of Reformation Christianity in general.[20] On the contrary, for Pole it was clear that
the denial of the primatial principle in fact abolishes the New
Testament structure and reinstates the exclusive claim of the
secular power. Accordingly, he says that Sampson "evidently
cannot imagine any other authority than that which can kill
the body and rob someone of his outward possessions".[21]
In the concrete case of England, the denial of the papacy
meant the transfer of the external order of the Church to
the state, that is, the state church system, and along with this
secular rule over the Church the simultaneous suppression
of *martyrium* (personal witness). Conversely, this meant (and
here we finally come to the real reason, which is psychological and at the same time theological, that caused Pole to become a defender of the papacy): the martyrs who countered
national Christianity subject to the crown with their faith
in the supranational unity of the universal Church and her
tradition were the guides who showed where the Christian
had to stand, as a Christian, in this conflict. This had two
consequences:

a. The martyrs and the theology of *martyrium* provided
Pole with an approach to the theology of primacy. Moreover,

Reginald Pole: Cardinal of England (London, 1950); D. Fenlon, *Heresy
and Obedience in Tridentine Italy: Cardinal Pole and the Counter-Reformation*
(Cambridge, 1971).

[20] Cf. Trimpe, *Macht aus Gehorsam*, chap. 11, sec. 2, p. 137, and p. 412,
n. 51.

[21] R. Pole, *Pro ecclesiasticae unitatis defensione libri quatuor* (Rome, un-
dated, ca. 1553–1554), 15 r 27 [= p. 15 recto, line 27].

he hit precisely upon the early Christian core of the theology of primacy, as it first becomes evident in John 21:18f. One can die only in person. The primacy as a testimony to the profession of faith in Christ is to be understood first in terms of the witness for which personal responsibility is taken in martyrdom, as the verification of one's witness to the Crucified who is victorious upon the Cross.

b. Against the background of such a theology of martyrdom/witness, the primacy figures essentially as the guarantee of the contrast between the Church in her catholic unity and the secular power, which is always particular.[22]

In this connection now we ought to ask, historically, what real content can be ascribed to Petrine theology if one does not view the Successor to Peter in the Bishop of Rome as its historical fulfillment. For those passages in the New Testament do exist and demand an explanation. Viewed historically, we can ascertain four answers, and it would hardly be possible to find any more; they exhaust the possibilities, although the details may vary.

The *first* answer is the Roman Petrine tradition.

The *second* answer was given by early fifth- and sixth-century Byzantine theology, which applied Matthew 16:16–19 and the whole plenipotentiary tradition that is connected with the name of Peter to the emperor; later this answer was hardly ever repeated in such an explicit form, but it reoccurs in fact wherever state-church structures are established.[23]

A *third* answer can be found in the writings of Theodore the Studite, although he does not propose it as an exclusive

[22] In these two points lies the specific thesis I intended to develop in this lecture—therefore, by no means a sort of "real utopia", as it seemed to many listeners.

[23] On this subject, see the material that A. Grillmeier has compiled in his essay "Auriga mundi", in *Mit ihm und in ihm*, 386–419, esp. 407.

solution to the problem. He sees the passages fulfilled in the monks, in the "spiritual men"[24]—a pneumatological solution, which has its importance as the inner dimension of the testimony, so to speak, but cannot exist by itself.

A *fourth* answer, for which Augustine supplied the prototype and which the Reformation took to its logical conclusion, sees the faith of the community as the *petra* (rock) in which the promises are fulfilled. But this interpretation does not do justice to the specific elements in these Gospel passages.[25]

So we have to say that the only remaining alternatives are the first and the second. But this means that either (as Pole puts it) full and absolute authority on earth has been granted to the state, or else the papacy, as in the "Roman" solution, is established as the powerless yet powerful entity confronting the secular power; the latter applies even when historically this led again and again to an attempt to clothe the powerlessness of this second "power" in worldly power, which obscured and endangered the Church's authentic character but could not dissolve it.

Let us return to Pole. With the martyrological approach,

---

[24] Cf. P. Kawerau, *Das Christentum des Ostens* (Stuttgart, 1972), 1077: "Later ages held Basil of Caesarea in such great esteem that he was called a second Peter. Theodore the Studite put it this way: 'You shone forth in the light of your brilliant life . . . ; but you yourself took up the keys like a new Peter and are the guardian of the whole Church.' Theodore was convinced that the monastic life founded by Basil was the foundation of the Church, and history to a great extent has confirmed that this conviction was correct."

[25] Cf. the comments of F. Mußner in "Petrusgestalt und Petrusdienst" and also his book *Petrus und Paulus—Pole der Einheit* (Freiburg, 1976). For the exegetical findings, see the essays by H. Zimmermann, R. Schnackenburg, G. Schneider, and J. Ernst in *Petrus und Papst*, ed. A. Brandenburg and H. J. Urban (Münster, 1977), 4–62.

we already have the basic answer to Sampson's question and ours: The vicariate of Christ is a vicariate of obedience and of the Cross; thus it is suited to the measure of man, and at the same time it surpasses him as much as being a Christian does in the first place.[26]

2. *Toward a concept of the primacy understood in martyrological terms*

What this means in practice becomes clearer if by way of example we select a few features from Pole's idea of the papacy while looking for elements of an answer to the question: What form should the papacy take today and in general? Indeed, as a candidate in a papal election, Pole was immediately confronted with this question, and we are in the historically unique position of having a record of the thoughts of a papal candidate in a conclave and of his own struggle with the prospect of taking on that task in a little book—*De summo Pontifice*—that he wrote during the conclave for his protégé, the youthful Giulio Cardinal de la Rovere.[27] In writing a sort of "mirror of the papacy", he intended to give him an aid to discernment, which endures as a monument to his own spiritual drama and offers us a point of departure for reflecting on the dimensions of the office by correctly outlining its features and at the same time revealing its deepest foundations.

What the pope should be and what he should be like is investigated in this book in strictly christological terms.

[26] Hence such a portrayal of the papal mission is as much or as little a utopia as any accurate depiction of the interior demands of being a Christian in general.

[27] R. Pole, *De Summo Pontifice Christi in Terris Vicario* (Louvain, 1569). For a thorough account of the composition and significance of this work, see Trimpe, *Macht aus Gehorsam*.

On the basis of what Christ is, it explains how and along what lines the pope should live out his task of "imitation", of succession and emulation. That which is a majestic title with reference to Christ (*laudes Christi*) is, with reference to the pope, a pattern for this required imitation.[28] In this way Pole approaches Isaiah 9:6f., a passage that was understood christologically in the Church's exegetical tradition, as a reflection of the papacy. Christ appears as a *parvulus natus* ("for to us a child is born"); christologically, this means that the Lord humbled himself for us, was obedient to the Father, and was sent by him. Christ, "the greatest", became for our sakes the *parvulus*, the "little one". Considered from the perspective of the imitation required of the pope, this means:

> When you hear that Christ was born and given as a child, apply this with reference to his Vicar to the latter's election: this is, so to speak, his birth. That means that you must understand that he is not born in this way for himself; he is not elected for his own sake, but rather for us, that is, for the whole flock. . . . In his ministry as shepherd, he must consider and conduct himself as one who is quite little and acknowledge that he knows nothing but this one thing: what he has been taught by God the Father through Christ (cf. 1 Cor 2:2).[29]

Pole says that the continuation of the prophecy, "the government will be upon his shoulder", refers to Christ, heavy laden for our sake; for him the dominant feature in this image is not the word "government", but rather the bearing of the superhuman burden on his human shoulders. The honorific title "Mighty Hero" is interpreted by the English Cardinal

[28] *De Summo Pontifice*, 27 r–v [recto-verso].
[29] Ibid., 28 v and 32 r–v.

in terms of what "might" or "strength" ultimately means in biblical language, and he finds a statement of this in the Song of Songs: "Love is strong as death" (8:6). The strength in which the Vicar of Christ must come to resemble his Lord is the strength of love that is ready for martyrdom.[30]

Among the titles to be analyzed here, Pole discovers a structure that connects the whole passage again with the point of departure previously outlined and brings to light the real heart of the matter: there are titles that can be described as titles of humility and lowliness (*parvulus natus, filius datus, principatus super humerum* [little Child, Son who is given, government upon his shoulder]), and titles of majesty (*magni consilii angelus, princeps pacis* [angel of great counsel, that is, "Wonderful Counselor", Prince of Peace], and so on). The two sets are irrevocably interrelated, first in Christ himself and, then, especially in the man who in the Christian faith is supposed to serve as his Vicar. The majestic titles pertain to Christ as *God* by nature; according to his *humanity*, however, he receives them only *after* his humiliation. Analogously, this is true for the representative: the majestic titles are effective and possible only in and by way of humiliation. The only way to participate in Christ's majesty is concretely through sharing in his lowliness, which is the sole form in which his majesty can be made present and represented in this time. Hence the authentic place of the Vicar of Christ is the Cross: being the Vicar of Christ is abiding in the obedience of the Cross and thus *repraesentatio Christi* in the age of this world, keeping his power present to counterbalance the power of the world . . .[31]

---

[30] Ibid., 52 r–v.

[31] Ibid., 55 r: ". . . nemo possit sequi Christum in iis quae ad gloriam spectant: nisi prius illum sequutus sit in eo, quod in hominum oculis nullam gloriae speciem obtinet." See also 43r: ". . . hanc praeclaram

Accordingly, with respect to Peter and consequently for the pope, Pole identified *sedes* (seat of authority, "Apostolic See") and "Cross". To Rovere's question, "How is the Chair of Peter, upon which the Vicar of Christ sits, similar to the Cross to which Christ was nailed?" he gives the following answer:

> That is not difficult for us to see, once we have understood that the Chair of the Vicar of Christ is the one that Peter established in Rome when he planted the Cross of Christ there. . . . During his entire pontificate he never descended from it, but rather, "exalted with Christ" according to the spirit, his hands and feet were fastened with nails in such a way that he wished, not to go where his own will urged him, but rather to remain wherever God's will guided him (cf. Jn 21:18), and his heart and mind were fastened there.[32]

The English Cardinal expresses it in the same way in another passage: "The office of the papacy is a cross, indeed, the greatest of all crosses. For what can be said to pertain more to the cross and anxiety of the soul than the care and responsibility for all the Churches throughout the world?" Moreover, he recalls Moses, who groaned under the burden of the whole Israelite people, could no longer bear it, and yet had to bear it.[33] To be bound up with the will of God, with the Word of whom he is the messenger, is the experience of being girt and led against his will of which John 21 speaks.

Christi personam . . . a nemine referri posse: qui non Christum ante in prioribus illis infirmitatis titulis . . . fuerit imitatus."

[32] Ibid., 132 v–133 r.

[33] Ibid., 133 v: ". . . munus ipsum Pontificatus Crucem esse et eam quidem omnium maximam. Quod enim magis ad Crucem et sollicitudinem animi (pertinere) dici potest, quam universarum orbis terrae Ecclesiarum cura atque procuratio?" Cf. ibid., 50 v 1.

Yet this attachment to the Word and will of God because of the Lord is what makes the *sedes* a cross and thus proves the Vicar to be a representative. He abides in obedience and thus in personal respons-ibility for Christ; professing the Lord's death and Resurrection is his whole commission and personal responsibility, in which the common profession of the Church is depicted as personally "binding" through the one who is bound . . .

This personal liability, which forms the heart of the doctrine of papal primacy, is therefore not opposed to the theology of the Cross or contrary to *humilitas christiana*[34] but rather follows from it and is the point of its utmost concreteness and, at the same time, the public contradiction of the claim that the power of the world is the only power and also the establishment of the power of obedience in opposition to worldly power. *Vicarius Christi* is a title most profoundly rooted in the theology of the Cross and thus an interpretation of Matthew 16:16–19 and John 21:15–19 that points to the inner unity of these two passages. No doubt, another facet of the bondage that in light of John 21 can be described as a definitive characteristic of the papacy will be the fact that this being bound up with God's will, which is expressed in God's Word, means being bound up with the "we" of the whole Church: collegiality and primacy are interdependent. But they do not merge in such a way that the personal responsibility ultimately disappears into anonymous governing bodies. Precisely in their inseparability, personal responsibility serves unity, which it will doubtless bring about the more effectively, the more true it remains to its roots in the theology of the Cross. Thus

---

[34] In this context, *humilitas* means humility, not simply as a moral virtue, but also as the objective recognition that righteousness is not the product of one's own efforts but, rather, the fruit of sanctifying grace.

Pole also defended the thesis that the man most suited to become the pope is the one who, from the perspective of a human choice of candidates, would be considered the least qualified in terms of the ideals of political shrewdness and executive power. The more a man resembles the Lord and thus (objectively) recommends himself as a candidate, the less human reason considers him capable of governing, because reason cannot fathom humiliation or the Cross.[35]

Conclusion: A View of the Situation in Christendom

Certainly it would be foolish to expect that in the foreseeable future a general unification of Christendom will occur around the papacy, understood as an acknowledgment of the Successor of Peter in Rome.[36] Perhaps it is also part of the necessary bondage and limitation of this commission that it can never be completely fulfilled and hence has to experience also the opposing presence of the Christian faithful, who expose whatever in him is not *vicarious* power but rather his own power. Nevertheless, even in this very way a unifying function of the pope extending beyond the communion of the Roman Catholic Church can become effective. Even in the opposition to the claim of his office, the pope personally remains in view of the whole world a point of reference with regard to the responsibility borne and expressed for the Word of faith, and thus he remains a challenge, noticed by

[35] *De Summo Pontifice* 79 r–v; 82 r; 90 r.

[36] Concerning the status of the ecumenical debate, see the study by F. Mußner mentioned in n. 25 and R. E. Brown, K. P. Donfried, and J. Reumann, eds., *Der Petrus der Bibel: Eine ökumenische Untersuchung* (Stuttgart, 1976), as well as a series of essays in the work by A. Brandenburg and H. J. Urban, *Petrus und Papst*, also mentioned in n. 25.

all and concerning all, to seek greater fidelity to this Word and, furthermore, a challenge to struggle for unity and to take responsibility for the lack of unity. In this sense, there is even in division itself a unifying function of the papacy, a function that in the final analysis no one can ignore in surveying the historical drama of Christendom. For the papacy and the Catholic Church, criticism of the papacy by non-Catholic Christians remains an incentive to seek an ever more Christlike actualization of the Petrine ministry; for non-Catholic Christians, in turn, the pope is the abiding, visible challenge to achieve the concrete unity to which the Church is called and which ought to be her identifying feature in the world's eyes. May we on both sides succeed in accepting without reservations the question that is posed to us and the task that is given to us and, thus, in obedience to the Lord, become that space of peace which prepares the new world—the kingdom of God.

Pope Paul VI receives a Token of Friendship [Freundeszeichen] *award from the Catholic Academy in Bavaria during the academic Symposium on "Service to Unity: On the Nature and Commission of the Petrine Ministry", which was organized by the Academy on the occasion of the Holy Father's eightieth birthday; Rome, October 11–14, 1977 (Photograph: Academy Archive/Felici).*

The Creed

A joint conference of the Evangelical-Lutheran Academy in Tutzing and the Catholic Academy in Bavaria, held April 1–3, 1966, in Tutzing on the theme "The Mission of the Church in the Non-Christian World" was the occasion for this lecture by Professor Joseph Ratzinger, then a professor of dogmatics and the history of dogma at the University of Münster. Theologians of both denominations posed the question about the central challenges facing Christianity in its relation to non-Christian religions in a world that is growing closer together.

THE PROBLEM OF THE ABSOLUTENESS
OF THE CHRISTIAN PATH TO SALVATION[1]

The experience of the relativity of all human realities and
of all historical arrangements is one of the characteristic intellectual certainties of our age: the encounter of mankind
with its history and the encounter of sectors of mankind that
had hitherto been living far apart from each other has set
not only the unity of mankind before our eyes in a moving
way, but also the relativity and historical dependence of all
human institutions and undertakings: everything that had
been considered unique finds its parallels all around, and
what had been taken as absolute appears in its connections
to its historical time. Christianity is not exempt from this
experience; it appears to be relativized, first, through the in-
significance of its historical extension and, secondly, by its
profound connection with the religious history of mankind
as a whole. This knowledge about the intertwining of Christianity with the spiritual and religious history of mankind,
in which its once special character is now scarcely visible
or even becomes utterly elusive, is one of the most urgent
questions of the Christian of our time. It has become a seemingly inescapable challenge to his faith: the discovery of the
relativizing breadth of history, which in a world grown small

---

Translated by Michael J. Miller.

[1] In keeping with the lecture format and the necessarily sketchy quality of these remarks, no effort has been made to cite scholarly sources
extensively.

presses us hard in an almost physical way, forms, together
with the discovery of the infinite breadth of the cosmos,
which seems to mock all anthropocentrism, the real catalyst
of the crisis of faith that we are facing. Therefore the question of the relation of Christianity to the world religions
has become today an intrinsic necessity for the faith: this is
not just an amusing curiosity that wishes to devise a theory about the destiny of others—that destiny is decided by
God, who does not need our theories; when it is merely a
matter of *that*, our questioning is idle, indeed, inappropriate.
But today more is at stake: the meaning of our own ability
and obligation to believe. The religions of the world have
become a question addressed to Christianity, which in their
presence must reconsider its own claim and thus receives
from them at least a service of purification, which already
in a rough outline allows us to glimpse how the Christian,
too, can understand such religions as necessary parts of salvation history.

But let us get to the topic itself, which of course is so
immense that no more than a few remarks on the subject
can be attempted here.

I. Remarks on the Question of the "Absoluteness" of Christianity

When we, following modern linguistic usage, describe the
Christian faith as "absolute", it is probably worthwhile first
to investigate the meaning and usefulness of this word.[2] Ety-
mologically it means "detached" and thus designates a reality that can exist in and of itself without another. It is clear

[2] Cf. H. Fries, "Absolutheitsanspruch des Christentums", *Lexikon für
Theologie und Kirche*, 171–74, with bibliography.

that such a statement would not be in agreement with the true claim of the Christian faith. It does not exist for itself but for something else and also in exchange with it; it comes from that something else, takes it up into itself, and thus also continues to carry it within, even though it is more than the product thereof and is essentially "new" with regard to it (the comparison with what happens in evolution suggests itself: man comes entirely from what went before, carries it within himself, and yet is essentially different from and more than that).

But then, "absolute" can also signify that something is not classified with other things under a common concept but, rather, stands alone. "Absoluteness" would then mean that the Christian faith is not classified together with other religions under a common generic concept of religion, so that the individual religions would be various sorts thereof. In fact, we allow ourselves again and again, more or less consciously, to be guided by the latter notion; indeed, even dogmatic theology to a large extent has fallen prey to it, for instance when it attempts to explain the nature of Christian sacrifice in terms of a general concept of sacrifice or the nature of priestly ministry in terms of a general understanding of priestly activity. Now of course an objection must be raised against such a view, not only for theological reasons, but first of all out of purely phenomenological considerations: the phenomena themselves allow no thoroughgoing, all-encompassing general concept of religion. For better or for worse, the philosophy of religion will renounce here the generalizing tendency of all philosophy and will have to accept the resistance of the phenomena, which cannot be assigned to a common genus. The atheistic religion of Buddhism balks at any common definition with the theistic types of religion in the West. And no one has the right to

call only the Western types "religion", which we are then
much inclined to do. Let us note the most obvious differences in a few catch-phrases that unavoidably oversimplify
the matter.[3] Theistic religion is "personally" directed, that
is, the pinnacle of being, the divine itself, is person; person
is an unsurpassable ultimate value that therefore cannot be
transcended again or taken up into something greater. For
most of Asian piety, in contrast, the Absolute is beyond the
personal; to cling to the latter would mean to perpetuate
the thirst for being that is the source of suffering; hence
transcending it, dissolving it into the pure "nothingness" of
pure being is the highest goal of the devotee. This already
suggests another contrast, which we could understand along
with Cuttat in terms of "separation" and "unity". In other
words, whereas for theistic thinking the indissoluble opposition of Creator and creature is a part of the unity that
love creates, for Asian mysticism the inseparable fusion into
an identity with the One, which is at the same time all, is
the only satisfactory goal of its striving toward the divine.
But where—this question now asserts itself—does Christian faith stand? Well then, it cannot be classified with Asian
identity mysticism; do we therefore have to look at it as a
variety of the Western type? This is a difficult question; it
would be premature to try to answer it already at this point.
In order to gain some orientation, allow us to anticipate
somewhat with a citation from the reflections on this question by J. A. Cuttat, which for the time being may stand

---

[3] For the following remarks I owe a debt of gratitude especially to the
studies by J. A. Cuttat, in particular *Begegnung der Religionen* (Einsiedeln,
1956). See also my essay "The Unity and Diversity of Religions", in
Truth and Tolerance: Christian Belief and World Religions, trans. Henry Taylor (San Francisco: Ignatius Press, 2003), 15–44. Further references can
be found there.

here without further clarifications; after several reflections we will return to it and then be able to evaluate it more closely. Cuttat views Christian faith as the unifying middle term between East and West when he says,

> At the point where Orient and Occident meet and separate, the Cross of the new Adam rises up. . . . Until the Incarnation, interiority and transcendence, spiritual infolding and unifying love, seemed to be divided by an insurmountable antinomy; apart from the Incarnation, the Orient and the Occident remained irreconcilable. "But when the time had fully come", the gulf proved to be bridged in the bosom of the triune life and passable in us too, because "God has sent the Spirit of his Son into our hearts, crying, 'Abba, Father!' "[4]

What was just said should at the same time make it clear that, in order to make any progress, we must look at the Christian claim more from the inside, even though the question with which we are concerned involves its outward relation to other religions. Let us start from the Old Testament. What is the decisive thing here in contrast to the religions of the nations? Certainly one could attempt to formulate it from various perspectives; let us try it—again only in outline form—in terms of the image of God. Then it would be possible to say: Yahweh, Israel's God, is not a *numen locale* of the sort that we find all around but, rather, a *numen personale*; not the god of a place, but God of men, the God of Israel, the God of the patriarchs. That means: in the midst of a world saturated with idols, where the mere word "god" says nothing and one must add something to specify which god is meant; where a name and a place are necessary to identify which one you are dealing with—in such a world, Israel's

---

[4] Cuttat, *Begegnung der Religionen*, 83f.

God identifies himself, not by a place, but by persons. He is not the god of Bethel, Sinai, or Canaan, but the God of the patriarchs: of Abraham, Isaac, and Jacob. By making this simple and seemingly quite ordinary observation, something critical is achieved, which decisively sets Israel's God apart from its environment in the history of religion: this god is not an immanent fertility force, a powerful condensation of the numinous mystery of the world; rather, he stands in lordly superiority over against the world. He is not bound to this place or that but, rather, is capable of helping his own wherever they are: he can protect Abraham's wife in Syria just as well as in Pharaoh's house; indeed, he can shield Cain all over the world from those who make attempts on his life. He gives his people Canaan, the land of the Baals, as their inheritance and can do this because the whole world belongs to him. The worshipper of Yahweh does not have to secure another deity as he travels from place to place; instead, wherever he is, Yahweh is powerful there to help him—for Yahweh is *his* God, the God of men.

Connected with this is another extremely important point: Yahweh, who is not a local god, therefore never became the god of the Jerusalem Temple, either, but was increasingly acknowledged as the global God who is free even to destroy the Temple—his temple! He never became the God of the promised land; rather, he remained the God who can distribute lands and is bound by none of them and needs none of them. He is not the god of fertility, a fruitful power of the earth, but, rather, the God of the universe who gives fruitfulness *also* . . . And that means finally and above all that he is not the ethnic god of Israel but, rather, the one God of the world, who can choose and reject peoples. Herein lies the almost heartrending paradox of Israel's religion, the fact that this people has the global God as their national God, that the national God of Israel is not a national God at all but, rather, precisely the non-national universal God who chose this people freely and lovingly yet is the God and Father of all peoples, indeed, the Creator of all peoples and of heaven and earth as well. One result of this, then, is the immense universalism of Israel's religion, which is the true substance of its "absolutism": not the dividing "Mother" earth, but, rather, the unifying and unique Father God is in the foreground—quite contrary to all thinking in antiquity. That signifies, however, the discovery of the unity of the humanity of all men, which Plato, for instance, did not find to be the case.[5] One could say much about this; here a reference to a few general points must suffice. Recall the idea of "Adam", who is man and mankind in one, a condensed expression of the fact that all men, however far away from one another they may grow to be, are and remain only "*one* man"; this idea is repeated once again in the figure of Noah and in the great table of nations in Genesis 10, which at the starting point of their division underscores the irrevocable unity of all. Moreover, we should recall the notion of the image and likeness of God endowed by creation, in which the loftier component of the identical humanity of all men becomes clear; in the story of Noah, this thought is taken up in the idea of establishing a covenant that is valid for all men. Finally, recent exegesis has clearly brought to light the universal historical significance of the Abraham narrative and of the "special salvation history" inaugurated in it: here mankind is not abandoned in favor of a particular election, but, rather, God starts with an individual so as then to win the whole.[6]

---

[5] Cf. J. Ratzinger, *The Meaning of Christian Brotherhood*, 2nd ed. (San Francisco: Ignatius Press, 1993), 5f.; J. Deissler, "Gott", in J. B. Bauer, *Bibeltheologisches Wörterbuch* (Graz, 1959), 352–68.

[6] Gerhard von Rad, *Old Testament Theology* (Westminster: John Knox Press, 2001), 1:135f.

Let us try to put together the results of these reflections!
Two things could be said on the basis of them.

a. Israel dared to worship the Absolute itself as the Absolute
One. Herein and here alone lies the total difference between
it and polytheism, and herein the decisive historical victory
over polytheism takes place.[7] For polytheism does not mean
maintaining that there is a multiplicity of the Absolute (as we
usually and naïvely assume); it is based instead on the notion
that it is unapproachable. And monotheism is distinguished
from polytheism, not by its recognition of the oneness of
the Absolute (this is a fundamental fact of human consciousness, to which even materialism adheres with its notion of
the absoluteness of matter); the difference lies instead in its
approachability and its own ability to speak. If one reflects
on this, one sees how close the modern consciousness is
to the basic presuppositions of polytheism, how much the
latter has become a temptation for all of us even today . . .

At this juncture, moreover, emerges the point of contact
between the polytheism of the ancient world and the Asian
religions, including Buddhism, which in many respects are
so different from them. For the religions of Asia, too (if
one may speak generically in this way), the divine Absolute
is suprapersonal or nonpersonal and, therefore, not the addressee of prescribed religious ceremonies, which it is incapable of perceiving and which it would therefore be senseless to devote to it. The prescribed religious acts can still
be offered, but only to the finite reflections of the Absolute, which represent it with relative purity and, hence, can
be called gods without being God (part of the definition of
gods, even for polytheism itself, is that they are not God).

[7] J. Ratzinger, *Der Gott des Glaubens und der Gott der Philosophen* (Munich and Zurich, 1960).

Because their addressee is only a penultimate thing, all these prescribed religious acts also can be only penultimate things themselves and not the ultimate. At this point, of course, Asian religiosity continued reasoning and decisively drew the conclusion that we will have to discuss next. Before we do, it should also be noted that, according to what has been said, the faith of Israel, whose peculiarity consists of worshipping the Absolute as the Absolute *One*, must at the same time have the peculiarity of worshipping God and *not* the gods: this very thing, after all, is its distinguishing characteristic. In other words, Israel's piety *must*, from its very outset, include the downfall of the gods. In this respect, the previously described positive absoluteness and universality of its faith necessarily and functionally entails a No to the gods, which cannot call themselves gods because they are not God. This state of affairs is the basis for the alliance between early Christianity and Greek enlightenment: Christianity perceives itself as a continuation of Greek philosophy, but not of the Greek religion, which it thoroughly denies and must deny.[8]

With these remarks we have outlined the special position of Israel's faith vis-à-vis the polytheism of the ancient world; the quite contemporary significance of it became evident in the latent polytheism of the present day. Precisely the question of the approachability of the Absolute, or of his own ability to speak, has become again the question separating Christian faith and the modern world, so that the real defining feature of the Christian claim and at the same time the polytheistic character of modern atheism have thereby come quite clearly into view. At the same time, this suggests

[8] The theology of religions that is coming into vogue today usually bypasses this state of affairs and thus misses the fundamental structure of the Christian faith.

a question that is important for missionary work (and for the theology of religions): the irrevocability of the downfall of the gods.

b. The Greek enlightenment and prophetic wisdom in Israel represent, each in its own way, an altercation with the problem of polytheism. At the same time, Asia addressed the same question in its own way in the Buddhist movement. In order to understand it, we must assume that polytheism itself (not only when it reached a stage of reflection, but somehow even in the so-called primitive religions with their peculiar combination of polytheism and monotheism) is aware that in the "gods" it does not worship "God", the real Absolute. From this then follows not uncommonly the insight that prescribed religious acts offered to the gods cannot be ultimate themselves but only penultimate, because their addressee is only penultimate. To this insight Asian religiosity adds: Prescribed religiosity as a whole is therefore only penultimate; the ultimate can only be negation, the pure No as a liberation from the penultimate and an entrance into the ultimate. With that a decision is now made about the Absolute that does not necessarily follow from the polytheistic beginning and is not found in Hellenism either: The world (and man with it and all personhood) is understood as the finite *appearance* of the infinite, appearance only and not being. This is where the turnabout occurs: if the world is only appearance, then ultimately it is not something separate or independent at all alongside the sole Absolute, which is the only reality. There remains the identity of a single true Being, from which only empty appearance separates us. In this way, of course, the contrast with Israel's faith is now fully and radically demonstrated: between Yahweh and his creature there is no identity, but only an "over-against" relation in word and response. And with that we have again reached our starting point, the question the ultimate character of the person, of the word.

And so the immediate relevance of these oppositions again becomes clear: identity, which at the same time involves relativizing the person and the word, includes the relativization of religious statements, so that they are merely symbolic: "One and the same moon is reflected in all waters. All moons in water are one in the one and only moon", as a metaphorical saying of Zen Buddhism puts it.[9] How well we understand all that! Again, how similar that is to the conceptual world of contemporary man, its recommendation of how Christians can finally resolve the religious problem. The faith of Israel is irreconcilable with such recommendations, and its indissolubility into such a harmony of symbols, which is based on the relativization of person and word, attains its full severity in the faith of Jesus Christ—whom we are now finally encountering: the fact that God is "over-against" us became fully irrevocable in the man Jesus; the God who wears a human face does not allow himself to be declared a suprapersonal One and All; his personhood and his speech have acquired an almost shocking concreteness. The fundamental Christian decision and the ineluctability of its claim to absoluteness, which is based on the absoluteness of the person, become unmistakably clear at this point.

c. Accordingly, the Christian renewal of the Old Testament signifies, first of all, that God's "being over-against", his personhood, is manifested with ultimate concreteness and reality in Christ.

And, nevertheless, although Christian faith makes the contradiction as acute as possible, there still occurs in it simultaneously a transcendence of the contradiction and an

[9] Cited in H. R. Schlette, *Colloquium salutis—Christen und Nichtchristen heute* (Cologne, 1965), 63.

overture to unity, albeit in an altogether different sense from
the symbolic universalism of Asia. For Christ signifies, not
only an "over-against" relation between God and man, but
rather union: union of man and God, union of man and man,
so radically that Paul—leaving Asiatic unity mysticism behind—can say, "You are all one in Christ Jesus" (Gal 3:28).
This brings us back to the remark by Cuttat from which we
started out: "At the point where Orient and Occident meet
and separate, the Cross of the new Adam rises up", who in
the Cross creates the interpenetration of two separate pieces
of wood, of two separated worlds. "For he is our peace, who
has made us both one, and has broken down the dividing
wall of hostility, . . . that he might . . . reconcile us both to
God in one body through the cross, thereby bringing the
hostility to an end" (Eph 2:14, 16).

II. On the Question of the Missions

At this point, where one could and should actually begin in
earnest now, I would like to and must interrupt these reflections on the question of the "absoluteness" of the biblical religion in order to make, in this second part, a few additional
no less fragmentary points on the question of the missions,
in other words, on the concrete relation of Christians to
other religions. We have seen that Christian "absolutism"
in terms of its content is a universalism that is based on
the universalism of Israel, which, transcending its national
boundaries, worships solely the God of the universe, the
"God of heaven", and thus first manages to break out of a
fenced-in nationality and unmasks as demons the gods that
banish men into it.[10]

[10] Cf. J. Ratzinger, "Menschheit und Staatenbau in der Sicht der frühen
Kirche", *Studium generale* 14 (1961): 664–82.

But now, in view of history, one must immediately ask: Does not this universalism turn out in practice to be, on the contrary, a massively exaggerated particularism that has been set up as absolute? The Jewish religion and, afterward, the Christian religion were the only ones incompatible with the Roman Empire, whereas the gods were in all respects interchangeable and could quite peacefully supplement one another in a great pantheon. Was it not precisely the universalism of Judaism or Christianity that first gave rise to the principle of intolerance in the history of religion, and is not this principle a necessary consequence of the Judeo-Christian form of universalism?[11]

Anyone who has carefully thought these questions through has sensed the need to add a clarification here, so as to make a distinction between the position of the religion of Israel and that of the Christian religion in history. Granted, the two have in common the fact that they could not be fit into Rome's pantheon: this necessarily follows from the basic form of their relation to God. But the Christian religion was the first to challenge polytheistic Rome on a larger scale to take up a militant attitude, because before the coming of Christianity, the latter had not felt threatened in its polytheism, which in antiquity was the fundamental principle of the State as such. The faith of Israel, for its part, did not fit into the ancient pantheon, but it did not really threaten it, either, and therefore could be tolerated (here *tolerance* really occurs for the first time; the interchangeability of the gods is based on the hidden fact that they are identical). This shows once again a decisive difference in the universalism shared by

---

[11] So argues H. von Glasenapp in various publications, for example, *Die fünf grossen Religionen* (Düsseldorf, 1952); Glasenapp, "Toleranz und Fanatismus in Indien", *Schopenhauer-Jahrbuch*, 1960. Worth noting as a corrective: P. Hacker, "Religiöse Toleranz und Intoleranz im Hinduismus", *Saeculum* 8 (1957): 167–79.

both, a difference that is decisive precisely for the question about the Church's approach to non-Christian religions. Although Israel was under orders to topple the gods in its own midst with the utmost determination and to worship God alone, it knew that it was not being commanded to topple the gods in general: that was God's business and his alone. And it knew that it was not being commanded to win over the nations for Yahweh-God: Yahweh had chosen Israel, although he was the father of all peoples, and had made it his "firstborn", "dearly beloved" son; the fact that he had not chosen the other peoples in the same way was not Israel's business and not really the business of the other peoples, either; only late Judaism then ascribes that to the guilt of the nations.[12] And so it could be the business of Yahweh alone to extend that election, just as it was solely his business to judge the "gods" (Ps 82[81]). Later, of course, the idea of a mission of Israel to the world of nations appeared, in the twofold form of the idea of suffering and the idea of light (a sign, a city on the hill). Yet here, too, salvation for the nations remains exclusively Yahweh's business, even though it now clearly enters the Jewish consciousness: history ends after Isaiah's splendid vision of the pilgrimage of the nations to Mount Zion (2:2). In this way, however, Israel's universalism remains a mere promise. It remains God's business, which Israel serves only through its obedient testimony of suffering and through the light that proceeds from this testimony of suffering. In other words: Israel's universalism remains "tolerant".

In the New Testament, a different picture emerges. According to the Christian faith, God himself entered into history in Christ; in him the last things have already begun,

---

[12] J. Ratzinger, *The Meaning of Christian Brotherhood*, 8f.

the end time is already here, and the pilgrimage of the nations to Mount Zion now becomes the pilgrimage of God to the nations. Universalism is no longer a mere vision of what is to come but, along with the faith that the end time is now, must be transformed into concrete facts—that is precisely the meaning of mission. The Church Fathers—following the lead of the New Testament—understand the Christ event as a mystery of union. Sin was separation into the egotism of each individual; it was "Babel", that is, the demolition of the bridge of understanding, the absolutizing of what was one's own in the individual and collective egotism of the nation and precisely therein—as a false, divisive absolutism—idolatry. In contrast, faith signifies a message about unity that transcends all boundaries and creates understanding across all boundaries in the one Spirit: "*One* Lord, *one* faith, *one* baptism, *one* God and Father of us all, who is above all and through all and in all" (Eph 4:5). One can understand the fascination that emanated from such a message, the hope that it aroused. But looking back at the history of Christianity, we cannot avoid a certain ambivalence at the thought of this message and of the attempts to put it into practice. Certainly, the proclamation of the unity of mankind and the endeavor to gain acceptance for it were and are something great—history received a new direction thereby, and we can no longer really imagine now what went before it. But anyone who professes it must not deny the danger and the fate of the whole business. The temptation to intolerance, to set up an unholy, this-worldly absoluteness that calls the other into question for time and eternity, becomes immense—and given the intellectual presuppositions of many periods in history, it appears virtually insuperable. What was once a promise now becomes—so it seems—a command: the salvation of others seems to depend no longer on divine mercy but, rather, on the success of the ecclesiastical endeavor. If that were the case, then one would of course have to call the idea of missionary work a terrible step backward from the simple, pure hope of Israel. (Here certainly is one reason why quite a few today—and not only the votaries of Ernst Bloch—become enthusiastic about the Old Testament as opposed to the New.)

In fact, it must be admitted that missionary work has to learn to understand itself better at this point—and of course that means in terms of the root of its inner meaning—than it has done until now. This is a major task for the modern theology of the missions. I would like to try to suggest briefly only two thoughts on the subject.

1. Although one can say in a certain sense that in matters of universalism the path from the Old Testament to the New Testament (or, more exactly, from Israel to the Church) is a path from promise to command (the missionary duty is a command that Israel did not know in that form), this partial perspective must necessarily be fit into the fundamental perspective according to which the path from the Old to the New Testament is precisely the reverse: a path from command to promise. After all, this is the content of the theology of Abraham that Paul presents in the fourth chapter of the Letter to the Romans, indeed, the core idea of Pauline preaching in general. Thus the command perspective is in any case subsumed under and subordinated to the promise perspective: command can exist only as an expression of the promise.

2. When one enters a bit deeper into the message of Jesus, into the context of the missionary command, and into the primordial Christian idea of mission in the first place, one

very soon sees that what has just been said not only constitutes a fundamental postulate resulting from the structure
of the Christian message, but also finds its illustration and
clarification in the will of Jesus.

The proclamation of Jesus was at first, not a proclamation
of the Church of the nations, but rather the announcement
of the kingdom of God, and thus in Jesus' own message universalism likewise remained pure promise, as J. Jeremias has
shown beautifully.[13] The exciting process, on which there
has been far too little theological reflection, that the Acts
of the Apostles depicts and that constitutes its real theological testimony, however, is as follows: Jesus' message about
the kingdom, which had met with its first rejection already
through the crucifixion of Jesus but was offered once more
after the Resurrection, was definitively rejected by Israel,
and from then on the message could exist only in the mode
of being en route to the nations. We call this being en route
of the message to the nations "Church". Out of that rejection of the message, which made it homeless and forced
it into being en route, arose the mission (which thus in a
very profound sense coincides with the Church herself);
it came into existence as the new form of the promise . . .
Consequently, mission as a form of Christian universalism
simply means that after the rejection of the kingdom (that
is, in the situation of an eschatologically not perfected but
sinful human race, which is signified for everyone in Israel's
No), the Word has no other homestead than being en route:
it shares the situation of the Son of man, who had nowhere
to lay his head (Mt 8:20). It shares the situation of the One
who is the Word, which came to his own home but was not
welcomed (Jn 1:11). Mission, accordingly, is an expression

---

[13] *Die Verheißung für die Völker*, 2nd ed. (Stuttgart, 1959).

for the earthly homelessness of the Word and, thus, precisely for the fact that it belongs to all.

I think a mission that increasingly understands itself in terms of these initial steps cannot be in opposition to universalism but rather, true to its etymological meaning, will be the expression thereof. And it cannot mean an antithesis to tolerance. The missionary idea shattered the congruence of religion and society that had hitherto been taken for granted, and thus the idea of freedom of religious profession was born in the first place in the blood of the martyrs—a freedom that is something different from the relativity and interchangeability of symbols for which it is generally mistaken nowadays.[14] Admittedly, what perversions history brought, how much guilt! And yet, thank God, its meaning was never extinguished. Figures like Las Casas, who fearlessly championed the powerlessness of the Word, have at no time been completely lacking in the missionary effort. And so, for all its weaknesses and all its failure, it nevertheless remained the conscience of the colonizers, the only brake on "colonialism", the refuge of what was humane in it. And it remained the leaven of the unification of mankind: commerce alone does not unite; only the Spirit can do that.

Nevertheless, in the end one might feel compelled to ask: Why missionary work, despite the promise that continues to exist? I think that we must answer: Missionary work exists, not *despite* the promise, but *on account of* the promise, as its powerless expression. It should allow itself to be deeply imbued with this element of promise, which does not abolish the command but makes it fearless. If we systematically inquire into the reasons for missionary work, then of course a lot of other things would have to be added. For instance,

[14] I have tried to explain this connection in more detail in my little book *Die letzte Sitzungsperiode des Konzils* (Cologne, 1966), 21.

the fact that it is necessary for the movement of history, for the sake of its unification. The fact that it must happen for the sake of the perpetual self-purification of Christianity, which can be accomplished only in the encounter with the other. The fact that it must exist because the others have a right to the message that has been entrusted to us, but from such a right follows our duty to witness, without our being thereby entitled to make the salvation of others dependent on the results of our efforts, which nevertheless are still our duty. Finally, we will have to admit that the Christian mission, too, at its deepest level, can desire nothing other than what was Israel's sacred duty: to be a light to the nations in its testimony of suffering and in its service of love. The pilgrimage of God to the nations, which is accomplished in missionary work, does not abolish the promise of the pilgrimage of the nations to God's salvation, which is the great light that shines out toward us from the Old Testament; it merely corroborates it. For the salvation of the world is in God's hand; it comes from the promise, not from the law. It remains for us to place ourselves humbly at the service of the promise, without wanting to be more than useless servants, who are doing only what is expected of them (Lk 17:10).

In the late 1960s, after the conclusion of the Second Vatican Council and in view of radical changes in society, the question about up-to-date ways of handing on the Christian faith became more acute. Therefore, under the provocative title "Outmoded Profession of Faith?", a joint conference of the Catholic Academy in Bavaria and the Evangelical-Lutheran Academy in Tutzing, held in Munich from March 22 to 24, 1968, dealt with this topic, which affects both of these Christian confessions. Collaborators on the Catholic side were Professor Joseph Ratzinger, who then occupied the chair for dogmatics on the Catholic theological faculty of the University of Tübingen, whose contribution is reprinted here, as well as Dr. Karl Lehmann, who at that time was an assistant professor at the University of Münster.

DIFFICULTIES WITH THE APOSTLES' CREED[1]

Descent into Hell—Ascension into Heaven—Resurrection of the Body

The following reflections do not aim to deal with the extensive questions concerning exegesis, the history of religion, the history of dogma, and hermeneutics that are connected with those bits of the Creed under discussion. That would be an excursion into a primeval forest, from which there would be no swift escape. They attempt, instead, to uncover the spiritual core of these respective statements in a meditative way and thus to lead to what the Creed is actually about, beyond all scholarship.

I. "Descended into Hell"

Possibly no article of the Creed is so far from present-day attitudes of mind as this one. Together with the belief in the birth of Jesus from the Virgin Mary and that in the Ascension of the Lord, it seems to call most of all for "demythologization", a process that in this case looks devoid of danger and

---

Translated by J. R. Foster; revised by Michael J. Miller.

[1] The text of this paper was taken from an explanation of the Apostles' Creed that was published in Autumn 1968 by Kösel-Verlag (Munich) under the title *Introduction to Christianity*. The sections on the Ascension and the resurrection of the body were accordingly abridged to fit the parameters of a lecture.

unlikely to provoke opposition. The few places where Scripture seems to say anything about this matter (1 Pet 3:19f.; 4:6; Eph 4:9; Rom 10:7; Mt 12:40; Acts 2:27, 31) are so difficult to understand that they can easily be expounded in many different ways. Thus if in the end one eliminates the statement altogether, one seems to have the advantage of getting rid of a curious idea, and one difficult to harmonize with our own modes of thought, without making oneself guilty of a particularly disloyal act. But is anything really gained by this? Or has one simply evaded the difficulty and obscurity of reality? One can try to deal with problems either by denying their existence or by facing up to them. The first method is the more comfortable one, but only the second leads anywhere. Instead of pushing the question aside, then, should we not learn to see that this article of faith, which liturgically is associated with Holy Saturday in the Church's year, is particularly close to our day and is to a particular degree the experience of our [twentieth] century? On Good Friday our gaze remains fixed on the crucified Christ, but Holy Saturday is the day of the "death of God", the day that expresses the unparalleled experience of our age, anticipating the fact that God is simply absent, that the grave hides him, that he no longer awakes, no longer speaks, so that one no longer needs to gainsay him but can simply overlook him. "God is dead and we have killed him." This saying of Nietzsche's belongs linguistically to the tradition of Christian Passiontide piety; it expresses the content of Holy Saturday, "descended into hell".

This article of the Creed always reminds me of two scenes in the Bible. The first is that cruel story in the Old Testament in which Elijah challenges the priests of Baal to implore their god to give them fire for their sacrifice. They do so, and naturally nothing happens. He ridicules them, just as the "enlightened rationalist" ridicules the pious person and finds him laughable when nothing happens in response to his prayers. Elijah calls out to the priests that perhaps they have not prayed loud enough: "Cry aloud, for he [Baal] is a god; either he is musing, or has gone aside, or he is on a journey, or perhaps he is asleep and must be awakened" (1 Kings 18:27). When one reads today this mockery of the devotees of Baal, one can begin to feel uncomfortable; one can get the feeling that *we* have now arrived in that situation and that the mockery must now fall on us. No calling seems to be able to awaken God. The rationalist seems entitled to say to us, "Pray louder, perhaps your God will then wake up." "Descended into hell"; how true this is of our time, the descent of God into muteness, into the dark silence of the absent.

But alongside the story of Elijah and its New Testament analogue, the story of the Lord sleeping in the midst of the storm on the lake (Mk 4:35–41, par.), we must put the Emmaus story (Lk 24:13–35). The disturbed disciples are talking of the death of their hope. To them, something like the death of God has happened: the point at which God finally seemed to have spoken has disappeared. The One sent by God is dead, and so there is a complete void. Nothing replies any more. But while they are there speaking of the death of their hope and can no longer see God, they do not notice that this very hope stands alive in their midst; that "God", or rather the image they had formed of his promise, had to die so that he could live on a larger scale. The image they had formed of God, and into which they sought to compress him, had to be destroyed, so that over the ruins of the demolished house, as it were, they could see the sky again and him who remains the infinitely greater. The German Romantic poet Eichendorff formulated the idea—

in the comfortable, to us almost too harmless fashion of his age—like this:

> *Du bist's, der, was wir bauen,*
> *mild über uns zerbricht,*
> *dass wir den Himmel schauen—*
> *darum so klag ich nicht.*[2]

Thus the article about the Lord's descent into hell reminds us that not only God's speech but also his silence is part of the Christian revelation. God is not only the comprehensible word that comes to us; he is also the silent, inaccessible, uncomprehended, and incomprehensible ground that eludes us. To be sure, in Christianity there is a primacy of the *logos*, of the word, over silence; God *has* spoken. God *is* word. But this does not entitle us to forget the truth of God's abiding concealment. Only when we have experienced him as silence may we hope to hear his speech, too, which proceeds in silence. Christology reaches out beyond the Cross, the moment when the divine love is tangible, into the death, the silence and the eclipse of God. Can we wonder that the Church and the life of the individual are led again and again into this hour of silence, into the forgotten and almost discarded article, "Descended into hell"?

When one ponders this, the question of the "scriptural evidence" solves itself; at any rate in Jesus' death cry, "My God, my God, why have you forsaken me?" (Mk 15:34), the mystery of Jesus' descent into hell is illuminated as if in a glaring flash of lightning on a dark night. We must not forget that these words of the crucified Christ are the opening

---

[2] Thou art he who gently
  breaks about our heads what we build,
  so that we can see the sky—
  therefore I have no complaint.

line of one of Israel's prayers (Ps 22:1 [21:2]), which summarizes in a shattering way the needs and hopes of this people chosen by God and apparently at the moment so utterly abandoned by him. This prayer that rises from the sheer misery of God's seeming eclipse ends in praises of God's greatness. This element, too, is present in Jesus' death cry, which has been recently described by Ernst Käsemann as a prayer sent up from hell, as the raising of a standard, the first commandment, in the wilderness of God's apparent absence: "The Son still holds on to faith when faith seems to have become meaningless and the earthly reality proclaims absent the God of whom the first thief and the mocking crowd speak—not for nothing. His cry is not for life and survival, not for himself, but for the Father. His cry stands against the reality of the whole world." After this, do we still need to ask what worship must be in our hour of darkness? Can it be anything else but the cry from the depths in company with the Lord who "has descended into hell" and who has established the nearness of God in the midst of abandonment by God?

Let us try to investigate another aspect of this complex mystery, which cannot be elucidated from one side alone. Let us first take account of one of the findings of exegesis. We are told that in this article of the Creed the word "hell" is only a wrong translation of *sheol* (in Greek, Hades), which denoted in Hebrew the state after death, which was very vaguely imagined as a kind of shadow existence, more nonbeing than being. Accordingly, the statement meant originally, say the scholars, only that Jesus entered *sheol*, that is, that he died. This may be perfectly correct, but the question remains whether it makes the matter any simpler or less mysterious. In my view it is only at this point that we come face to face with the problem of what death really is, what happens when someone dies, that is, enters into the fate of death. Confronted with this question, we all have to admit our embarrassment. No one really knows the answer because we all live on this side of death and are unfamiliar with the experience of death. But perhaps we can try to begin formulating an answer by starting again from Jesus' cry on the Cross, which we found to contain the heart of what Jesus' descent into hell, his sharing of man's mortal fate, really means. In this last prayer of Jesus, as in the scene on the Mount of Olives, what appears as the innermost heart of his Passion is not any physical pain but radical loneliness, complete abandonment. But in the last analysis what comes to light here is simply the abyss of loneliness of man in general, of man who is alone in his innermost being. This loneliness, which is usually thickly overlaid but is nevertheless the true situation of man, is at the same time in fundamental contradiction with the nature of man, who cannot exist alone; he needs company. That is why loneliness is the region of fear, which is rooted in the exposure of a being that must exist but is pushed out into a situation with which it is impossible for him to deal.

A concrete example may help to make this clearer. When a child has to walk through the woods in the dark, he feels frightened, however convincingly he has been shown that there is no reason at all to be frightened. As soon as he is alone in the darkness, and thus has the experience of utter loneliness, fear arises, the fear peculiar to man, which is not fear of anything in particular but simply fear in itself. Fear of a particular thing is basically harmless; it can be removed by taking away the thing concerned. For example, if someone is afraid of a vicious dog, the matter can be swiftly settled by putting the dog on a chain. Here we come up against something much deeper, namely, the fact that where man falls into extreme loneliness he is not afraid of anything definite that could be explained away; on the contrary, he experiences the fear of loneliness, the uneasiness and vulnerability of his own nature, something that cannot be overcome by rational means. Let us take another example. If someone has to keep watch alone in a room with a dead person, he will always feel his position to be somehow or other eerie, even if he is unwilling to admit it to himself and is capable of explaining to himself rationally the groundlessness of his fear. He knows perfectly well in his own mind that the corpse can do him no harm and that his position might be more dangerous if the person concerned were still alive. What arises here is a completely different kind of fear, not fear of anything in particular, but, in being alone with death, the eeriness of loneliness in itself, the exposed nature of existence.

How then, we must ask, can such fear be overcome if proof of its groundlessness has no effect? Well, the child will lose his fear the moment there is a hand there to take him and lead him and a voice to talk to him; at the moment therefore at which he experiences the fellowship of a loving human being. Similarly, he who is alone with the corpse will feel the bout of fear recede when there is a human being with him, when he experiences the nearness of a "You". This conquest of fear reveals at the same time once again the nature of the fear: that it is the fear of loneliness, the anxiety of a being that can only live with a fellow being. The fear peculiar to man cannot be overcome by reason but only by the presence of someone who loves him.

We must examine our question still further. If there were such a thing as a loneliness that could no longer be penetrated and transformed by the word of another; if a state of abandonment were to arise that was so deep that no "You" could reach into it any more, then we should have real, total loneliness and dreadfulness, what theology calls "hell". We can now define exactly what this word means: it denotes a loneliness that the word love can no longer penetrate and that therefore indicates the exposed nature of existence in itself. In this connection who can fail to remember that writers and philosophers of our time take the view that basically all encounters between human beings remain superficial, that no man has access to the real depths of another? According to this view, no one can really penetrate into the innermost being of someone else; every encounter, beautiful as it may seem, basically only dulls the incurable wound of loneliness. Thus hell, despair, would dwell at the very bottom of our existence, in the shape of that loneliness which is as inescapable as it is dreadful. As is well known, Sartre based his anthropology on this idea. But even such an apparently conciliatory and tranquilly cheerful poet as Hermann Hesse allows the same thought to appear in his work:

> *Seltsam, im Nebel zu wandern!*
> *Leben ist Einsamsein.*
> *Kein Mensch kennt den andern,*
> *Jeder ist allein!*[3]

In truth—one thing is certain: there exists a night into whose solitude no voice reaches; there is a door through which we can only walk alone—the door of death. In the last analysis all the fear in the world is fear of this loneliness. From this point of view, it is possible to understand why the Old Testament has only one word for hell *and* death, the word *sheol*; it regards them as ultimately identical. Death is

---

[3] Curious, to walk in a mist!
Life is loneliness.
No man know his neighbor,
Everyone is alone!

absolute loneliness. But the loneliness into which love can no longer advance is—hell.

This brings us back to our starting point, the article of the Creed that speaks of the descent into hell. This article thus asserts that Christ strode through the gate of our final loneliness, that in his Passion he went down into the abyss of our abandonment. Where no voice can reach us any longer, there is he. Hell is thereby overcome, or, to be more accurate, death, which was previously hell, is hell no longer. Neither is the same any longer because there is life in the midst of death, because love dwells in it. Now only deliberate self-enclosure is hell or, as the Bible calls it, the second death (Rev 20:14, for example). But death is no longer the path into icy solitude; the gates of *sheol* have been opened. From this angle, I think, one can understand the images— which at first sight look so mythological—of the Fathers, who speak of fetching up the dead, of the opening of the gates. The apparently mythical passage in Saint Matthew's Gospel becomes comprehensible, too, the passage that says that at the death of Jesus tombs opened and the bodies of the saints were raised (Mt 27:52). The door of death stands open since life—love—has dwelt in death.

II. "He Ascended into Heaven and Is Seated at the Right Hand of the Father"

To our generation, whose critical faculty has been awakened by Bultmann, talk of the Ascension, together with that of the descent into hell, conjures up that picture of a three-story world which we call mythical and regard as finished with once and for all. "Above" and "below", the world is everywhere just world, governed everywhere by the same physical laws, in principle susceptible everywhere of the same kind of investigation. It has no stories, and the concepts "above" and "below" are relative, depending on the standpoint of the observer. Indeed, since there is no absolute point of reference (and the earth certainly does not represent one), basically one can no longer speak at all of "above" and "below"—or even of "left" and "right"; the cosmos no longer exhibits any fixed directions. No one today will seriously contest these discoveries. There is no longer such a thing as a world arranged literally in three stories.

But was such a conception ever really intended in the articles of faith about the Lord's descent into hell and Ascension to heaven? It certainly provided the imagery for them, but it was just as certainly not the decisive factual element in them. On the contrary, the two tenets, together with faith in the historical Jesus, express the total range of human existence, which certainly spans three metaphysical dimensions if not three cosmic stories. To that extent it is only logical that the attitude that at the moment is considered "modern" should dispense not only with the Ascension and the descent into hell but also with the historical Jesus, that is, with all three dimensions of human existence; what is left *can* only be a variously draped ghost, on which—understandably—no one any longer wishes to build anything serious.

But what do our three dimensions really imply? We have already come to see that the descent into hell does not really refer to any outer depths of the cosmos; these are quite unnecessary to it. In the basic text, the prayer of the crucified Christ to the God who has abandoned him, there is no trace of any cosmic reference. On the contrary, this article of the Creed turns our gaze to the depths of human existence, which reach down into the valley of death, into the zone of untouchable loneliness and rejected love, and thus embrace the dimension of hell, carrying it within themselves as one of their own possibilities. Hell, existence in the definitive rejection of "being for", is not a cosmographical destination but a dimension of human nature, the abyss into which it reaches down at its lower end. We know today better than ever before that everyone's existence touches these depths; and since in the last analysis mankind is "*one* man", these depths affect not only the individual but also the one body of the whole human race, which must therefore bear the burden of them as a corporate whole. From this angle it can be understood once again how Christ, the "new Adam", undertook to bear the burden of these depths with us and did not wish to remain sublimely unaffected by them; conversely, of course, total rejection in all its unfathomability has only now become possible.

On the other hand, the Ascension of Christ points to the opposite end of human existence, which stretches out an infinite distance above and below itself. This existence embraces, as the opposite pole to utter solitude, to the untouchability of rejected love, the possibility of contact with all other men through the medium of contact with the divine love itself, so that human existence can find its geometrical place, so to speak, inside God's own being. The two possibilities of man thus brought to mind by the words heaven and hell are, it is true, completely different in nature and can be quite clearly distinguished from each other. The depths we call hell man can only give to himself. Indeed, we must put it more pointedly: Hell consists in man's being unwilling to receive anything, in his desire to be self-sufficient. It is the expression of enclosure in one's own being alone. These depths accordingly consist by nature of just this: that man will not accept, will not take anything, but wants to

stand entirely on his own feet, to be sufficient unto himself.
If this becomes utterly radical, then man has become the
untouchable, the solitary, the reject. Hell is wanting only to
be oneself; what happens when man barricades himself up
in himself.

Conversely, it is the nature of that upper end of the scale
which we have called heaven that it can only be received, just
as one can only give hell to oneself. "Heaven" is by nature
what one has not made oneself and cannot make oneself;
in Scholastic language it was said to be, as grace, a *donum
indebitum et superadditum naturae* (an unowed gift added over
and above nature). As fulfilled love, heaven can always only
be granted to man; but hell is the loneliness of the man who
will not accept it, who declines the status of beggar and
withdraws into himself.

Only from this standpoint does it become clear now what
is really meant in the Christian view by heaven. It is not
to be understood as an everlasting place above the world
or simply as an eternal metaphysical region. On the contrary, "heaven" and "the Ascension of Christ" are indivisibly connected; it is only this connection that makes clear
the christological, personal, history-centered meaning of the
Christian tidings of heaven. Let us look at it from another
angle: heaven is not a place that, before Christ's Ascension,
was barred off by a positive, punitive decree of God's, to
be opened up one day in just as positive a way. On the
contrary, the reality of heaven only comes into existence
through the confluence of God and man. Heaven is to be
defined as the contact of the being "man" with the being
"God"; this confluence of God and man took place once and
for all in Christ when he went beyond *bios* through death
to new life. Heaven is accordingly that future of man and

of mankind which the latter cannot give to itself, which is therefore closed to it so long as it waits for itself, and which was first and fundamentally opened up in the man whose field of existence was God and through whom God entered into the creature "man". Therefore heaven is always more than a private, individual destiny; it is necessarily connected with the "last Adam", with the definitive man, and, accordingly, with the future of man as a whole.

III. "The Resurrection of the Body"

1. *The content of the New Testament hope of resurrection*

The article about the resurrection of the body puts us in a curious dilemma. We have discovered anew the indivisibility of man; we live our corporality with a new intensity and experience it as the indispensable way of realizing the one being of man. From this angle we can understand afresh the biblical message, which promises immortality, not to a separated soul, but to the whole man. Such feelings have in this century made Lutheran theology in particular turn emphatically against the Greek doctrine of the immortality of the soul, which is wrongly regarded as a Christian idea, too. In reality, so it is said, this idea expresses a thoroughly un-Christian dualism; the Christian faith knows only of the waking of the dead by God's power. But doubts arise at once here: The Greek doctrine of immortality may well be problematical, but is not the biblical testimony still more incapable of fulfillment for us? The unity of man, fine, but who can imagine, on the basis of our present-day image of the world, a resurrection of the body? This resurrection

would also imply—or so it seems, at any rate—a new heaven
and a new earth; it would require immortal bodies needing
no sustenance and a completely different condition of matter. But is this not all completely absurd, quite contrary to
our understanding of matter and its modes of behavior, and
therefore hopelessly mythological?

Well, I think that in fact one can only arrive at an answer if one inquires carefully into the real intentions of the
biblical testimony and at the same time considers anew the
relation between the biblical and the Greek ideas. For their
encounter with each other has modified both conceptions
and thus overlaid the original intentions of both approaches
with a new combined view that we must first remove if we
want to find our way back to the beginning. First of all, the
hope for the resurrection of the dead simply represents the
basic form of the biblical hope for immortality; it appears in
the New Testament not really as a supplement to a preceding
and independent immortality of the soul but as the fundamental statement on the fate of man. There were, it is true,
in late Jewish teachings hints of immortality on the Greek
pattern, and this was probably one of the reasons why very
soon the all-embracing scope of the idea of resurrection in
the Graeco-Roman world was no longer grasped. Instead,
the Greek notion of the immortality of the soul and the
biblical message of the resurrection of the dead were each
understood as half the answer to the question of the fate
of man, and the two were added together. It was thought
that, to the already existing Greek foreknowledge about the
immortality of the soul, the Bible added the revelation that
at the end of the world bodies would be awakened, too, to
share henceforth forever the fate of the soul—damnation or
bliss.

As opposed to this, we must grasp the fact that originally it was not a question of two complementary ideas; on the contrary, we are confronted with two different outlooks, which cannot simply be added together: the image of man, of God, and of the future is in each case quite different, and thus at bottom each of the two views can only be understood as an attempt at a total answer to the question of human fate. The Greek conception is based on the idea that man is composed of two mutually foreign substances, one of which (thc body) perishes, while the other (the soul) is in itself imperishable and therefore goes on existing in its own right independent of any other beings. Indeed, it was only in the separation from the body, which is essentially foreign to it, so they thought, that the soul came fully into its own. The biblical train of thought, on the other hand, presupposes the undivided unity of man; for example, Scripture contains no word denoting only the body (separated and distinguished from the soul), while conversely in the vast majority of cases the word soul, too, means the whole corporeally existing man; the few places where a different view can be discerned hover to a certain extent between Greek and Hebrew thinking and in any case by no means abandon the old view. The awakening of the dead (not of bodies!) of which Scripture speaks is thus concerned with the salvation of the *one*, undivided man, not just with the fate of one (perhaps secondary) half of man. It now also becomes clear that the real heart of the faith in resurrection does not consist at all in the idea of the restoration of bodies, to which we have reduced it in our thinking; such is the case even though this is the pictorial image used throughout the Bible. What, then, is the real content of the hope symbolically proclaimed in the Bible in the shape of the resurrection of the dead? I think that this can best be worked out by means of a comparison with the dualistic conception of ancient philosophy.

1. The idea of immortality denoted in the Bible by the word "resurrection" is an immortality of the "person", of the *one* creation "man". Whereas in Greek thought the typical man is a perishable creature, which as such does not live on but goes two different ways in accordance with its hetero-geneous formation out of body and soul, according to the biblical belief it is precisely this being, man, that as such goes on existing, even if transformed.

2. It is a question of a "dialogic" immortality (= awaken-ing!); that is, immortality results not simply from the self-evident inability of the indivisible to die but from the saving deed of the lover who has the necessary power: man can no longer totally perish because he is known and loved by God. All love wants eternity, and God's love not only wants it but effects it and is it. In fact the biblical idea of awakening grew directly out of this dialogical theme: he who prays knows in faith that God will restore the right (Job 19:25ff.; Ps 73:23ff.); faith is convinced that those who have suffered in the interests of God will also receive a share in the redemp-tion of the promise (2 Macc 7:9ff.). Immortality as con-ceived by the Bible proceeds, not from the intrinsic power of what is in itself indestructible, but from being drawn into the dialogue with the Creator; *that is why* it must be called awakening. Because the Creator intends, not just the soul, but the man physically existing in the midst of history and gives *him* immortality, it must be called "awakening of the dead" = "of men". It should be noted here that even in the formula of the Creed, which speaks of the "resurrection of

the body", the word "body" means in effect "the world of man" (in the sense of biblical expressions like "all flesh will see God's salvation", and so on); even here the word is not meant in the sense of a corporality isolated from the soul.

3. That the awakening is expected on the "Last Day", at the end of history, and in the company of all mankind indicates the communal character of human immortality, which is related to the whole of mankind, from which, toward which, and with which the individual has lived and hence finds salvation or loses it. At bottom this association results automatically from the collective character of the biblical idea of immortality. To the soul as conceived by the Greeks, the body, and so history, too, is completely exterior; the soul goes on existing apart from them and needs no other being in order to do so. For man understood as a unity, on the other hand, fellowship with his fellowmen is constitutive; if *he* is to live on, then this dimension cannot be excluded. Thus, on the biblical premise, the much-discussed question of whether after death there can be any fellowship between men seems to be solved; at bottom it could only arise at all through a preponderance of the Greek element in the intellectual premises: where the "communion of saints" is an article of faith, the idea of the *anima separata* (the "separated soul" of Scholastic theology) has in the last analysis become obsolete.

The full elaboration of these ideas became possible only after the New Testament had given concrete shape to the biblical hope—the Old Testament by itself ultimately leaves the question about the future of man in the air. Only with Christ, the man who is "one with the Father", the man through whom the being "man" has entered into God's eternity, does the future of man definitely appear open. Only in him, the "second Adam", is the question of man's identity finally answered. Christ is man, completely; to that extent the question of who we men are is present in him. But he is at the same time God speaking to us, the "Word of God". In him the conversation between God and man that has been going on since the beginning of history has entered a new phase: in him the Word of God became "flesh" and really gained admission into our existence. But if the dialogue of God with man means life, if it is true that God's partner in the dialogue himself has life precisely through being addressed by him who lives forever, then this means that Christ, as God's Word to us, is himself "the resurrection and the life" (Jn 11:25). It also means that the entry into Christ known as faith becomes in a qualified sense an entry into that being known and loved by God which is immortality: "Whoever believes in the Son *has* eternal life" (see Jn 3:15; 3:36; 5:24). Only from this angle is it possible to understand the train of thought of the fourth evangelist, who in his account of the Lazarus episode wants to make the reader understand that resurrection is not just a distant happening at the end of the world but happens now through faith. Whoever believes is in the conversation with God that is life and that outlasts death. At this point, too, the "dialogic" strand in the biblical concept of immortality, the one related directly to God, and the "human fellowship" strand meet and join. For in Christ, the man, we meet God; but in him we also meet the community of those others whose path to God runs through him and so toward one another. The orientation toward God is in him at the same time toward the community of mankind, and only the acceptance of this community is movement toward God, who does not exist apart from Christ and thus not apart either from the context of the whole history of humanity and its common task.

This also clarifies the question, much discussed in the patristic period and again since Luther, of the "intermediate state" between death and resurrection: the existence with Christ inaugurated by faith is the start of resurrected life and therefore outlasts death (see Phil 1:23; 2 Cor 5:8; 1 Thess 5:10). The dialogue of faith is itself already life, which can no longer be shattered by death. The idea of the sleep of death that has been continually discussed by Lutheran theologians and recently also brought into play by the Dutch Catechism is therefore untenable on the evidence of the New Testament and not even justifiable by the frequent occurrence in the New Testament of the word "sleep": the whole train of thought of every book in the New Testament is completely at variance with such an interpretation, which could hardly be inferred even from late Jewish thinking about the life after death.

2. *The essential immortality of man*

The foregoing reflections may have clarified to some extent what is involved in the biblical pronouncements about the resurrection: their essential content is not the conception of a restoration of bodies to souls after a long interval; their aim is to tell men that they, they themselves, live on; not by virtue of their own power, but because they are known and loved by God in such a way that they can no longer perish. In contrast to the dualistic conception of immortality expressed in the Greek body-soul schema, the biblical formula of immortality through awakening means to convey a collective and dialogic conception of immortality: the essential part of man, the person, remains; that which has ripened in the course of this earthly existence of corporeal spirituality and spiritualized corporeality goes on existing in a different fashion. It goes on existing because it lives in God's memory. And because it is the man himself who will live, not an isolated soul, the element of human fellowship is also part of the future; for this reason the future of the individual man will only then be full when the future of humanity is fulfilled.

A whole series of questions arises at this point. The first is this: Does this view not make immortality into a pure grace, although in reality it must fall to man's lot by virtue of his nature as man? In other words, does one not finish up here with an immortality only for the pious and, thus, in a division of human fate that is unacceptable? To put it in theological terms, are we not here confusing the natural immortality of the being "man" with the supernatural gift of eternal love that makes man happy? Must we not hold fast, precisely for the sake of the humanity of the Christian faith, to natural immortality, for the reason that a continued existence conceived in purely christological terms would necessarily slide into the miraculous and mythological? This last question can indubitably be answered only in the affirmative. But this is by no means at variance with our original premise. It, too, entitled us to say decisively: The immortality that, precisely because of its dialogic character, we have called "awakening" falls to the lot of man, *every* man, as man, and is not some secondary "supernatural" addition. But we must then go on to ask: What really makes man into man? What is the definitive distinguishing mark of man? To that we shall have to answer: The distinguishing mark of man, seen from above, is his being addressed by God, the fact that he is God's partner in a dialogue, the being called by God. Seen from below, this means that man is the being that can think of God, the being opened onto transcendence. The point here is not whether he really does think of God, really does open himself to him, but that he is in principle the being who is in himself capable of doing so, even if in fact, for whatever reasons, he is perhaps never able to utilize this capacity.

Now one could say: Is it not, then, much simpler to see the distinguishing mark of man in the fact that he has a spiritual, immortal soul? This definition is perfectly sound; but we are in fact at this moment engaged in the process of trying to elucidate its concrete meaning. The two definitions are not in the least contradictory; they simply express the same thing in different modes of thought. For "having a spiritual soul" means precisely being willed, known, and loved by God in a special way; it means being a creature called by God to an eternal dialogue and therefore capable for its own part of knowing God and of replying to him. What we call in substantialist language "having a soul" we will describe in a more historical, actual language as "being God's partner in a dialogue". This does not mean that talk of the soul is false (as is sometimes asserted today by a one-sided and uncritical biblical approach); in one respect it is, indeed, even necessary in order to describe the whole of what is involved here. But, on the other hand, it also needs to be complemented if we are not to fall back into a dualistic conception that cannot do justice to the dialogic and personalistic view of the Bible.

So when we say that man's immortality is based on his dialogic relationship with and reliance upon God, whose love alone bestows eternity, we are not claiming a special destiny for the pious but emphasizing the essential immortality of man as man. After the foregoing reflections, it is also perfectly possible to develop the idea out of the body-soul schema, whose importance, perhaps even indispensability, lies in the fact that it emphasizes this essential character of human immortality. But it must also be continually put back in the biblical perspective and corrected by it in order to remain serviceable to the view of man's future opened up by faith. For the rest, it becomes evident once again at this point that in the last analysis one cannot make a neat distinction between "natural" and "supernatural": the basic dialogue that first makes man into man makes a smooth transition into the dialogue of grace known as Jesus Christ. How could it be otherwise if Christ actually is the "second Adam", the real fulfillment of that infinite longing that arises from the first Adam—from man in general?

Conversing with Professor Walter Kasper during the academic Symposium on "Service to Unity: On the Nature and Commission of the Petrine Ministry", which was organized by the Catholic Academy on the occasion of the eightieth birthday of Pope Paul VI; Rome, October 11–14, 1977 (Photograph: Academy Archive/Felici).

What salvation does faith offer? For what does it hope? And what is the relation between Christian hope and those political and social perspectives on the future that have their basis in this life? These questions were dealt with in a highly acclaimed evening program, "This-Worldly and Christian Hopes of Salvation" on September 26, 1974, in Munich. The talk by Dr. Joseph Ratzinger, at that time professor of dogmatics and the history of dogma at the University of Regensburg, takes up a position from a theological perspective. The other talk that evening was given by Dr. Ulrich Hommes from a philosophical viewpoint.

THE SALVATION OF MAN—
THIS-WORLDLY AND CHRISTIAN

Salvation—Happiness—Future

In the course of its development, the word "salvation" (*Heil*) has increasingly withdrawn from everyday language into the house of theology, and to the same extent it has lost its significance and importance for the average sensibility. The word "happiness" appeared at first as its successor. But that could capture only a part of what salvation had once expressed: it designates only the well-being of the subject, of the individual, and excludes the world, which was in the field of vision with the term salvation. The slant of its meaning runs almost in the opposite direction from that of salvation. The idea of "salvation" implies that the world is "redeemed" and, consequently, that I am, too; in using the word happiness, my thought is that I am content with my "quality of life" and with the world, at any rate to the extent that it has treated me well. Nevertheless, in the word "happiness", too much had been left out for it to be able in the long run to serve as a valid replacement for "salvation", and thus a second word moved to the fore, which along with "happiness" divides up the former rights of "salvation" and in so doing ridicules or even insults the little word "happiness" as being petit bourgeois. I mean the words "hope" and "future", which exert an increasingly powerful fascination,

---

Translated by Michael J. Miller.

because they promise something greater than "happiness" could ever mean.

In a sense, this rehabilitates the intention behind the word "salvation", but its theological content is rejected perhaps even more than before. The assertions of the faith had already been rather burdensome for "happiness"; just a few years ago I read in an indictment of the Church by a former priest the statement that with her prohibitions she has disputed our right even to the "little bit of happiness" that life grants frugally enough in the first place. At first, salvation, shrunken to the form of "saving the soul", could continue to live in an adjoining room of human existence, but even in this case "saving the soul" and "happiness" were usually perceived as opposites, and however much one might take away from his "happiness" for the benefit of "saving his soul", the relationship between the two generally remained somewhat tense. But now, to the extent that saving the soul was put on a starvation diet, so to speak, an unexpected development ensued. The more "happiness" was understood as being against the "soul" and therefore allowed itself greater freedom, the more voracious and pale it became at the same time. Since he had nothing left ahead of him, the man hungry for happiness had to insist all the more on being able to have, now and unconditionally, whatever he wanted; yet the more barriers he tore down, the more considerable the remaining ones became for him. The comparison with the greater happiness of someone else who had nevertheless not deserved it more increasingly became a gloomy shadow that darkened even what had been attained; only complete equality could present itself as hope, and of course it could take its measure only from the most sublime possibilities, for only there could be supplied what was so missing to oneself. In order to achieve this, the alliance of all the disadvantaged appeared to be the only path, and consequently a moral duty of exciting proportions once again emerged; morality, at first shoved aside into the individual realm of saving the soul, privatized and tormented as an everlasting opponent of happiness, appeared now in a new form as a task for mankind as a whole: to bring about the salvation of the world in a union with all the disenfranchised; in comparison, personal happiness could seem to be only a shallow substitute or middle-class narrow-mindedness. The makeable future—the time of total freedom and equality—now clothed itself in all the literal and emotional connotations of "salvation" and "happiness" at once.

In this light, theological particulars from former times appear even more disagreeable and useless than they did under the modest lamp of bourgeois happiness. What previously might have been considered the final justification of this matter of faith advocated by theology becomes now the principal accusation: namely, the fact that it was a stabilizing factor in the world and society, which held things and people together tolerably well. For by that very fact, one must now admit, it hindered the emergence of a better world and defended things that ought not to have been defended but rather destroyed. By consoling people with the hope of saving their souls, it dulled the contradictions of the present world, deprived it of its severity, and thus brought people to the point where they coped with the world as it is now, instead of stirring them up to fight for a better one. By making the world seem bearable to people, or perhaps by actually making it somewhat bearable by one good deed or another, it did not do good but, rather, postponed the radical change for the better and thus favored those who had reason to fear that awakening. So now, in every respect, the exact opposite of what the Christians wanted and did must be done. Instead of remembering God's good works, the potential of the "dangerous memory" must be awakened, all the bad memories of history must be brought back and driven home, so that the pent-up force of this consciousness of evil might sweep away the dams that protect today's world. Instead of urging people to practice charity, which binds up wounds, helps in small ways, and thus makes it possible to put up with great privations, one must now intensify to the utmost their awareness of inequity. "Raising consciousness" replaces charity: the naked, unsparing knowledge—gnosis —of the world's cruelty: this must provide explosives in sufficient quantity to bring down the walls that separate and to bring in the new. Today practically no one can exclude himself any more from this program. Certainly one hears voices calling for resignation, precisely from those thinkers who at first were in the vanguard of the new movement—the later writings of [the German social philosopher] Horkheimer, for instance, who finally found the inhumanity of technological society no less cruel than the misery of religious society, so that the only way left for him to conceive of man's fate was through the perspective of tragedy. While resignation may be the wisdom of old age, it is not an attitude with which to build a life. No wonder theology, too, tried, with varying degrees of zeal, to participate in the work of constructing a new world, for if there is finally some prospect of the world ceasing to be a valley of tears, then who could possibly stand aloof? Today, actually, the question is not at all whether or not one participates in the program of the makeable future or manipulates hope in the laboratory (to modify an expression of Ernst Bloch); the question is really about what instruments one will use and from what directions one will aim at the goal. A man who in response to the question about salvation does not speak about the future and offers no strategy by which the world can be changed fundamentally has in the opinion of most contemporaries said nothing at all substantial in any way—that is, unless they label him a reactionary who wants to conserve the world in its present state.

It is characteristic of reason, however, to contradict, to inquire about particulars, to critique. It is up to reason to oppose the prevailing opinion. The empirical facts that the ideologues and technicians of the future have to adduce reinforce this drive to question everything. But the basic thought pattern that is predominant here must call forth opposition, also. Just in passing, let us list a few questions that arise when one overcomes the anaesthetization of reason that results from the fascinating dream of the future world. Can indignant consciousness, can the hatred fomented by remembering evil, bring about equality among men? Or does it not necessarily continue to be omnipresent as envy, poisoning people? Can the destruction of the present really lead to higher ground and a better future? Can happiness, "salvation", be produced at all through the redistribution of this-worldly goods? On what do happiness and unhappiness really depend? What concepts of salvation and ruin (*Heil und Unheil*) are being applied by someone who discards the charitable gesture and the resulting tolerability of life because he would be satisfied only by a world in which he no longer needed this gesture? Is man correctly understood by someone who wants to ensure happiness collectively and is certain about the badness of the past because he finds fault with its societal model? Can the fate of the people who went before us, the value and disvalue of what they believed, hoped, and loved, be measured against the economic parameters of industrialized society? Yes, they have their contradictions, which are unmistakably the product of the technological-economic rationale set loose by the Enlightenment, but can we simply write them off as the end product of previous history? Can we act as though the peoples of the Third World, while still living in immense misery, are nevertheless gradually experiencing a somewhat better lot thanks to the work of the envoys of Western technological reason and Eastern revolutionary reason, when in fact it is precisely these two new forms of "missionary work" in the first place that are producing their specific type of misery, which rightly disturbs us?

Now let us not question things generally but instead ask quite concretely about ourselves. What about us—what really makes life worth living for a person today? The prospect that there will be a more equitable world in fifty years? That may be a passion that gives some meaning, one that challenges and keeps us going. But is this enough? Is it not in reality precisely the opinion that the world could someday be in order that makes life today unbearable and hopeless? Does it not create a fanaticism that devastates life? In extrapolating salvation into the future, does not life become dull and gloomy, does not declaring love and humor heretical destroy the real prerequisite for the future? Several odd yet quite typical observations about the human condition today should be considered in this connection: What is the real cause for the fact that there is less and less room for children —for the future of mankind—in our society? How are we supposed to explain the fact that, for professional reasons, some now want to treat the child—the future—as a sickness and have it "cured" (that is, killed)? What strange reversal of the will to future lies in the fact that now all our energies should be focused on how to deal most quietly and safely with the "risk" of new life?

Of course there are many reasons for this—first, a sort of agoraphobia when confronted with calculations about the limits of growth, which lead one to try to defend one's own place in the world and to fear the future as the enemy of today. But perhaps we must look deeper. Behind this, ultimately, is there not a concern about whether human life can be undertaken at all, whether it is a meaningful gift that one can confidently and unquestioningly hand on, or whether it is not actually an unbearable burden, so that it would be better not to be born? Who answers this question, which in the midst of the apotheosis of the future makes a person ever more deeply insecure? The strategists for a new world? Certainly not. For the question of whether it will be worthwhile tomorrow to be a human being does not depend on the mode of distributing goods but, rather, on deeper questions that haunt man, even if they are not publicly named.

The first task that is important today for the conscientious person (and so for the theologian, also) must be to awaken slumbering reason. The answer of faith has not become unintelligible because of the keenness of reason but, rather, on account of its exhaustion. Someone whose thinking ends with statistics can find little that is useful in the faith of Christians. The poverty of today's theology seems to me to be based in no small measure on the fact that it lacks the courage to awaken reason in its entirety. But where this is neglected, the only alternative remaining is either to proclaim what is totally unintelligible or else to adapt to the prevailing mood. But then an informative talk about Christianity secretly becomes an excuse that does not actually provide a justification for the Christian faith but at least makes the theologian in question look like a sensible contemporary with whom one can reason. In the long run, of course, one will make no progress along this path whereby theologians try to save their skin at the price of proclaiming all of Church history anathema. For what is the "reasonableness" of an individual theologian worth if the cause for which he speaks has followed an unreasonable course until now? If theology is to have any meaning beyond the self-validation of the theologian, then the private reasonableness of its proponents must not first be shown, but instead the theologian must first of all simply, in a workmanlike way, so to speak, give information about what the faith teaches, without which there would be no theologian. This by no means contradicts what was said previously: The faith needs reason in order to be understood and put into practice. But in this instance, it needs above all a kind of reason that not only tries to be productive but can also perceive what confronts it. It needs a reason that listens. And that is why the beginning of all theology is first to give listening its due and to accept the data as it is given, even if it runs contrary to our momentary expectations. The great opportunities of the future always come from what we have not foreseen.

The Answer from the Sources of the Faith

Let us take up, therefore, the question that the modern mentality to a great extent has left behind, namely: About what kind of salvation does faith really speak? So as not to have to pursue our discussion beyond all bounds, it will be a good idea to delimit it as precisely as possible and to restrict it, even though much of the breadth of the topic will necessarily be lost. Our formulation of the question aims throughout at the contrast between this-worldly and Christian expectations concerning salvation. This suggests that, in contrast to the secular hope for the future that has been discussed so far, we now ask what sort of hope faith actually has to offer. What does man have to hope for according to the message of the New Testament? In keeping with our earlier reflection, we ourselves intend to try initially to listen to the information in the documents without commentary and, so to speak, as literally as possible. Of course, the objection will immediately arise that such an attempt can lead only to hermeneutical naïveté, for what one detects in a text already depends, after all, on how one questions it and on how one comes to an understanding of it. That is correct. And yet, it cannot be that the identity of the faith is completely hidden in the clouds of hermeneutics. The faith itself claims to be simple and a message specifically for simple people. The faith itself protests against the idea that only "gnosis", an erudite knowledge, can convey it and that someone not instructed in hermeneutics must forever remain at the level of the *psychikos*, the ultimately clueless person. The faith itself has resisted efforts to encode it in the language of specialists, a process that began as early as the first century, by holding up the Creed as the simple hallmark (*symbolum*) of its identity. Only because it is simple can it reach what is most profound and hence be explicated again and again and never be fully measured. Only what is simple is immeasurable; the path from something complicated leads no farther, unless it is by way of a fresh return to simplicity. Thus, without denying the immeasurable character of the faith, we may certainly begin with simple listening. I am selecting a text with which Paul defends the old Palestinian profession of faith in its unabridged and undiminished claim to reality against the *sophia*, or learned wisdom, of the Corinthians, so as to address in detail this question: Where is the Christian actually going, and on what basis does he build his life?

> If Christ has not been raised, then our preaching is in vain and your faith is in vain. We are even found to be misrepresenting God, because we testified of God that he raised Christ, whom he did not raise if it is true that the dead are

not raised. For if the dead are not raised, then Christ has
not been raised. If Christ has not been raised, your faith
is futile. . . . Then those also who have fallen asleep in
Christ have perished. If for this life only we have hoped
in Christ, we are of all men most to be pitied. . . . If the
dead are not raised, "Let us eat and drink, for tomorrow
we die." Do not be deceived: "Bad company ruins good
morals." Come to your right mind, and sin no more. For
some have no knowledge of God. I say this to your shame.
(1 Cor 15:14–19, 32–34)

The answer given here is plain: The Christian hopes for
the resurrection of the dead. This must first be said unambiguously, even though today it may sound naïvely mythical and there are all sorts of pressure to weaken the statement by interpreting and transforming it, even before it is
formulated. If the statement is not made, then one has already set out on the path of evasion. For Paul, the meaning
of the Christian proclamation depends on *this* expectation;
without it, faith and proclamation are null and void to him
and Christian life is senseless.[1] In the history of dogma, this
statement has developed in two ways:

a. Included in the conviction about the resurrection of the
dead is the expectation of a new heaven and a new earth,
that is, the certainty that there will be a positive fulfillment
of the meaning of cosmos and history, the certainty that the
two do not end as a rubbish heap that finally and indiffer-
ently lays the blood and tears of this age to rest as empty illu-

[1] Although it cannot be discussed here, for a treatment of the question
of how the "resurrection of the dead" can be understood appropriately
in terms of the text and in light of current knowledge, I refer to my
Introduction to Christianity (San Francisco: Ignatius Press, 2000), 347–95.

sions.[2] The image of "the new heaven and the new earth" sees at the end, rather, an overall meaning into which all partial meanings enter. They are "taken up" into it and belong to it, but it is not the sum or the product of them. Precisely this reduction of reality to the contrast of material and product, which occurred in the philosophy of the modern era and was carried over into the practice of the technological age, has become the doom of man, who for the first time completely experiences therein the contradiction between willing and work. Under the universal rule of this pattern of thought and life, something that is not a product, and hence is not to be brought forth by calculated effort, appears to us as altogether insignificant. And yet hope in its true sense first appears when we have something to expect beyond our own production. To this extent, the reference to the new heaven and the new earth is an acknowledgment that man may hope in the first place, and only this then gives meaning to his productions as well.[3]

b. In the history of dogma, a second aspect has been expressed with ever greater clarity, namely, that the Christian promise also includes that individual personal fulfillment into which life after death flows. This was expressly formulated in the year 1336 by Pope Benedict XII in his Bull *Benedictus Deus*: "The souls of . . . [the] faithful who [have] died . . . provided they were not in need of any purification

---

[2] Cf. J. Ratzinger, *Dogma und Verkündigung* (Munich, 1973), 301–14; *Dogma and Preaching* (San Francisco: Ignatius Press, 2011), 260–71.

[3] Cf. R. Schaeffler, *Die Religionskritik sucht ihren Partner* (Freiburg, 1974), esp. 47–57, where these problems are discussed in a very illuminating way under the title "Jenseitskritik und Ressentimentverdacht" (Criticism of the next world and the suspicion of ill will).

. . . before they take up their bodies again and before the general judgment . . . are . . . in heaven . . . and see the divine essence . . . face to face."[4] It must be said quite clearly: The Christian expects heaven—even today. In a world that is acquainted with the law of the conservation of energy, it does not surprise him that the mysterious energy that we call "spirit" or "soul" is not lost and finally sees through all the shadows to its ground of being, communicates with it and, precisely thereby, with the whole of creation.

In this connection, another incidental remark is necessary. In referring to the question that death poses for every human hope, we mentioned "heaven" but did not speak about hell, which is not a "hope" but rather the end of hope and, in that respect, the radicalization of the phenomenon of death. Still it is worth mentioning that the noted sociologist P. L. Berger, in searching for a new, inductive justification for belief in transcendence—in God—brings the "argument of damnation" into play:

> This refers experiences in which our sense of what is humanly permissible is so fundamentally outraged that the only adequate response . . . seems to be a curse of supernatural dimensions. . . . What concerns me is not how Eichmann is to be explained or how Eichmann should have been dealt with. . . . For here is a case . . . in which condemnation can be posited as an absolute and compelling necessity. . . . A refusal to condemn in absolute terms would appear to offer prima facie evidence not only of a profound failure in the understanding of justice, but more profoundly of a fatal impairment of *humanitas*.[5]

[4] Denzinger-Schönmetzer, *Enchiridion Symbolorum*, 32nd ed. (Freiburg, 1963), nos. 1000–1002; cf. my article "Benedictus Deus", in *LThK* 2: 171ff.

[5] Peter L. Berger, *A Rumor of Angels: Modern Society and the Rediscovery of the Supernatural* (Garden City, N.Y.: Doubleday, 1970), 65–66.

Once again: Christian hope is called heaven; if Christian doctrine also knows the word "hell", that means that Christian hope is certainty of true justice, which can also be a curse when a human life is injustice down to the roots.

In view of such particulars, which are established by the original documents of the faith, there is no avoiding the question: But does that mean nothing is promised for this world, for this time? That leads us to a third observation:

c. Hope for some definitive progress in history and for a definitively sound society within history is nowhere part of Christian expectation. The idea of progress did develop out of Christianity, but as a notion of a this-worldly increase in well-being that can be made collective and permanent, it is itself not Christian. The date of its origin can be rather clearly determined: it is found in the work of the Calabrian abbot Joachim of Fiore (ca. 1130–1202), who projected the Christian belief in the Trinity onto history and accordingly expected an ascending line of history from the age of the Father (Old Testament) through the age of the Son (New Testament) to the age of the Holy Spirit. The pious monk, who was himself the founder of a religious order and is honored as Blessed, still saw this future entirely from the perspective of the faith, indeed, of monasticism: the age of the Spirit was supposed to bring about at last the complete observance of the Sermon on the Mount, the reconciliation of Latins and Greeks, of Jews and Christians; it was supposed to be an age of monks in which everyone would live the life that Benedict and the great founders of religious orders had anticipated in an exemplary way in the age of the Son.[6] Ernst Benz has traced the steps by which this idea was

[6] Cf. my article "Joachim v. Fiore", in *LThK* 5:975f. and the bibliography there.

transformed from a pious expectation into a secular political program; via Hegel the perspective of the simple abbot became a force that continues to shape history to this very hour.[7] Moreover, even Joachim was no stranger to the idea that it is possible to play into the hands of the future, to work for its coming, to prepare for it and to help bring it about; his own religious foundation understood itself to be an attempt to anticipate the future in this way.

We can understand very well this transformation of the profession of faith in the Trinity into a stepwise logic of history: After all, discontent with the existing world has always awakened a longing for the Golden Age; after the waning of the expectation of Christ's immediate return, the discrepancy between the prophetic promises of the Old Covenant and the Church of actual reality necessarily evoked such outlines of a true Church and a definitively redeemed world. The Church, nevertheless, rejected them as a misunderstanding of her profession of faith during the dramatic controversy of the thirteenth and fourteenth centuries, and she was quite right to do so. The Christian expectation for this world is to be described quite differently in terms of the Bible and the underlying articles of faith. For the Bible, this world will always be a world of affliction and toil. In order to substantiate this statement, we need not resort to the Book of Revelation, for this conviction is one of the constant messages of the whole New Testament. It is formulated perhaps most strikingly in the farewell discourses of Jesus in the Gospel of John. The last sentence before the so-called High-Priestly Prayer reads: "I have said this to you, that in me you may have peace. In the world you have tribulation; but be of good cheer, I have overcome the world" (Jn 16:33).

[7] Cf. the account of Joachim's later influence by E. Benz, *Ecclesia spiritualis* (Stuttgart, 1934); K. Löwith, *Weltgeschichte und Heilsgeschehen*, 3rd ed. (Stuttgart, 1953), esp. 136-47.

Nowhere is there talk about progress that has been or could be established collectively. Nevertheless, there is also an earthly promise for faith, which admittedly looks quite different from the expectations for the future that date from Joachim. The Gospel of Mark records for us Peter's question: What will be the reward for the total renunciation of the disciples who for Jesus' sake have given up everything? Jesus answers with an enigmatic saying that still expresses in an astonishing way the intertwining of faith's hope and earthly happiness, the connection between "this" world and "the next": "Truly, I say to you, there is no one who has left house or brothers or sisters or mother or father or children or lands, for my sake and for the gospel, who will not receive a hundredfold now in this time, houses and brothers and sisters and mothers and children and lands, with persecutions, and in the age to come eternal life" (Mk 10:29–30). What is that supposed to mean? Now it is plain that this statement immediately concerns the missionary, who in proclaiming the Word and building up the Church receives again a hundredfold what he gave up: everything is his because nothing is his; in the midst of persecution, hostility, and tribulation, he is nonetheless wealthy and gifted beyond human expectation. The logic that in the Old Testament was applied to the tribe of Levi, to the priests, is transferred here to the missionary of Jesus Christ. The tribe of Levi received no land; its allotment was "only" God; the right of priests is modeled on the right of the poor.[8] But precisely in this way he is rich: because nothing in particular belongs to him, everything belongs to him. Accordingly, this saying is about the specific situation of the man who sets out on a journey for the Word (*das Wort*) and in the poverty of the Word experiences the wealth of the answer (*der Ant-wort*).

[8] Cf. H. J. Kraus, *Psalmen* (Neukirchen, 1960), 1:118–27 (= commentary on Ps 16).

Nevertheless, one may indeed say that this also expresses a fundamental connection between faith's renunciation and a kind of fulfillment that reaches into this world as well, which of course is clearly situated in the context of persecution. Earthly hardship is not abolished, and yet there is also in this world a corroboration of the promise that abides in faith.

With his brother Georg at the reception hosted by the Catholic Academy on the occasion of his ordination as Archbishop of Munich and Freising: May 28, 1977 (Photograph: Academy Archive/Gerd Pfeiffer).

The Objection: Empty Promise?

The data in the original documents, which is thus outlined in broad strokes within the limitation that has been set, automatically presses at this point beyond itself to the question: What does all this mean? What does it mean for us here and now? Well, the answer to the initial question about the hope of the Christian is at first quite clear: The Christian hopes for eternal life. Anyone who overlooks or disputes this is no longer speaking about the Christianity of the New Testament but rather about his own inventions, which have no authority and no relevance. So after all is said and done, *summa summarum*, the next world is an empty promise, someone will now immediately object. I think that here we must first, before any further reflections and so as to make them possible, simply reject the expression "empty promise", for several reasons:

a. First we must be allowed to respond with a question of our own: Who is actually promising? What, then, is an "empty promise"? Someone will answer: The kind of promise that changes nothing. The opposite of an empty promise is a deed, a change that makes consolation superfluous. But is that really the case? If a person does begin to change society but can promise success in fifty years at best, is he not offering an empty promise? Whom then does his change benefit? Even assuming that it will be successful (although everything suggests the contrary), does it help, for instance, the person who is suffering now? And what does the change actually cost? What sacrifices are put up with, what form of destruction, not only externally, but in and to man himself? Kasimir Edschmid, in his novel about Bolivar, depicted in sensational images the enormous extent of the spiritual, physical, and economic destruction that the South American war of independence from the Spaniards caused, down to its tragic conclusion, in which Bolivar, pursued by his own government, died in the house of a Spaniard. Supposedly that battle was unavoidable. But were not the ones who had to live through it betrayed most despicably and given "empty promises", since the only results of their battle, after all the devastation, were the lacerated nation states of the subcontinent, whose poverty distresses us today? Yet we do not need to go back one hundred fifty years. In his novel *August 1914*, Aleksandr Solzhenitsyn captured with almost photographic accuracy the creed of those who believe in the future in a short dialogue between a military doctor and an enlightened ensign concerning the first to be wounded in the war. "Individual instances of so-called compassion", the ensign says to the astonished doctor, "only obscure the issue and postpone a general solution. The worse things are in this war and the worse things are for Russia, the better!" The doctor objects, "You mean it doesn't matter if wounded Russian soldiers are tormented by fever and in delirium? If they get infected? . . . Let them suffer, let them die, so much the better—is that what you're saying?" In response to his objection, the doctor is instructed: "You have to look at the whole picture and see things in perspective if you don't want to make a fool of yourself. There is not and never was a shortage of suffering in Russia! Let the sufferings of the wounded be added to the sufferings of the workers and peasants. The scandalous lack of facilities for treating them is a good thing because it brings the end so much nearer. The worse, the better!"[9] Anyone who has ever spoken with people who believe in the future knows that this dialogue is

[9] *August 1914: The Red Wheel/Knot I*, trans. H. T. Willetts (New York: Noonday Press, Farrar Straus & Giroux, 1989), 121–22.

not invented. It reveals the true intellectual background of the *Gulag Archipelago*: the reader of this novel senses what suffering it cost, slowly to recognize that this sign of horror did not come about despite the battle for a better future and against empty promises but, rather, was precisely its product and its exact expression.

Anyone who investigates such connections will find that opposition between empty promise and change necessarily collapses. For him the makeable future will cease to be the true concept of salvation. Helmut Kuhn recently described very precisely the fascinating and destructive character of belief in a makeable world: "Moreover, what is modern and yet to come is 'good' for those who believe in the future, because history is progress, being good means being progressive, and evil is anything reactionary. The vertical dimension is replaced by the horizontal. The imperative is no longer *Sursum corda!* (Lift up your hearts!), but rather: Be avant-garde! The past is what you must emancipate yourself from; the present is the object of social criticism; the future—that which is not or is not yet—is everything. It is activated nothingness—the parasitical spider that, as long as it still has an appetite, covers reality with ideological webs and snares."[10]

b. The reference to eternal life is certainly coupled with realism, which unmasks any collectively established progress of humanity as a mirage and contrasts it with the factuality of a world in which one must fight again and again for humanity and where it will always be difficult to be a human being. But another part of this realism, resulting from the conviction about the reality of what is eternal, is the conviction that it will nevertheless always be *possible* to be a

[10] H. Kuhn, "Zukunftsmusik", in *Notwendige Bücher: H. Wild zum 65. Geburtstag* (Munich, 1974), 55.

human being, precisely because heaven exists, which is by no means only the future but, rather, a reality of the utmost importance at present. In that respect, an empty promise is not being offered here at all; instead the empty promises are removed, and people are led to existence in reality.

c. The reference to "heaven" is not an empty promise if the eternal life of which we are talking is a reality. Then one must not remain silent about it. Then everything really is different; the significance of each individual step in human life is then changed. The question involved here is so important that one cannot exclude it so as to do something more urgent for the time being. The *question*, at least, tolerates no suppression. And if praxis is a criterion of truth, then precisely in this instance it gives a weighty answer. The more the passion for eternal life was awakened in men, the more "human" and humanizing they became. The dynamism of the saints can be understood only in terms of the new gravity that broke into their life and changed its dimensions from the ground up. For all the terrible things that Church history has to show, one thing is clear: destruction and indifference did not come from those who were really filled with faith in eternal life. From Benedict via Francis of Assisi to Bartolomé de las Casas, Peter Claver, and Vincent de Paul, the real believers are the rays of hope that taught mankind what being human could be; they are the great consolers who did not offer empty promises but, rather, healing. Perhaps it is helpful, besides the reference to those great figures who made heaven visible on earth and thus made the earth habitable, to cite a perhaps rather abstruse yet quite typical example of how the appearance of the eternal at the margin of life was able to offer a little consolation even in places where social criticism was warranted. When

Duke Ludwig the Bearded of Bavaria-Ingolstadt sensed that death was drawing near in the year 1434, he realized "that much had been lacking in his life; that ill-gotten gains stuck to his fingers; that the means he had employed had not always been the right ones or even permissible. Only constant prayer, he thought, could save him now—prayer that had to come from the poor to whom the kingdom of heaven is promised. And so he founded an almshouse for fifteen poor people who, as long as the world continued, were to live there on his inheritance and pray for him."[11] The medieval anxiety about the next world, which finds expression in such testaments, has often been ridiculed. But would it not have been good if it had appeared, not just at the end, but also in the middle of life? The fear of some—the fear that justice is a reality, a power—was the hope of others, and the fact that fear became hope in them was also able to transform the fear of those who had good reason to be afraid.

Eternity as the Present

Such reflections pave the way for an answer to the question: What does it really mean "to expect eternal life"? What does it mean when a man believes in and hopes for life everlasting? After all, this is not just any item contained in his consciousness in the way that all sorts of knowledge are contained therein and also disappear again; rather, it shapes spiritual existence from its beginning, and it thereby shapes it with regard to others, also. Here I would like to venture the thesis: Whether there is any happiness at all (in *this* life!) for a man depends on the existence of eternal life. The hope

[11] B. Hubensteiner, *Ingolstadt Landshut München: Der Weg einer Universität* (Regensburg, 1973), 13.

of eternal life does not put off salvation until much later, far from it! It is, on the contrary, the prerequisite for the possibility of there being any well-being or "salvation"—something like happiness—in the first place. How so? Well, if there is no eternity, if spirit is not the prior, creative element but rather a subsequent, chance occurrence, then the real *as such* has no meaning. Nor can man change anything fundamental about it. For he himself is then also, as such, a construct without meaning. In limited contexts he can set up circles of meaning, so to speak, without, however, being able to change thereby the quality of the whole. For being as such, reality as a whole, is not changed by such productions. The particular meaning produced is then, after all, a form of playing in and at absurdity. But that is not a matter of indifference for human life, either. Here and there it can flee into the particular figures of meaning that it brings forth. But since in its foundation it extends down into meaninglessness, the power of absurdity will remain the decisive thing in the depth of all thought, being, and action. Robert Spaemann has persuasively demonstrated how such a division of meaning and being (*Sinn und Sein*) leaves man with only two alternatives: becoming a fanatic or a cynic.

> The fanatic finds himself in a meaningless facticity and sides with meaning, with love, communication, and reason against reality. Whether there is any meaning at all depends on his action. And therefore, as he pursues his goal, no moral standards whatsoever are set for him, since his goal is what establishes morality in the first place. His failure would be the worst of all evils, because the world-as-it-is is the worst of all possible worlds. The antithesis of the fanatic is the cynic. Meaning, reason, happiness are for him epiphenomena on the surface of a meaningless facticity. Whether as an active player or as a satisfied onlooker, he sides with this facticity, with power against

meaning, which is only an illusion. For him, as for the fanatic, everything is permitted, except that he needs no justification for it from morality or the history of philosophy. Fanaticism and cynicism are opposites, yet they meet, like all extremes. The cynic is often a disillusioned fanatic who has lost faith that his goal can be realized and now no longer seeks meaning but only power.[12]

But how does it look on the political level? Have we not escaped into the personal, private realm and by this renunciation actually shown partiality for the position of those who have power now and thus tacitly sided with them? Now the dilemma described by Spaemann does extend quite deep into political decisions, which cannot be divorced from the fundamental decision about the meaning and absurdity of the world. Thus in the political sphere, we face an alternative that reflects and continues the opposition of cynicism and fanaticism. The controversy in recent years has shaped a very clear opposition in this regard. On the one side, value-free positivistic rationality raises its hand to speak, trying to judge and act according to the immanent objectivity of the field in question. On the other side stands that critique of all that exists which measures the world by the standard of a dominion-free society of total freedom and equality and, on that basis, condemns the alleged objectivity as disguised special interest and arrives at such a radical critique of the status quo that it must condemn reforms as "reformism" and views the mobilization of all forces for total change as the only way to well-being and salvation. Although the passion for "justice" and "freedom" is seductive, the dogmatism that measures the present against illusory pictures of the future and destroys it because of them is necessarily

---

[12] R. Spaemann, "Die Frage nach der Bedeutung des Wortes 'Gott'", *Internationale katholische Zeitschrift "Communio"* 1 (1972): 54–72, citation at 71.

intimidating. The flight into pure objectivity, into pure rationality suggests itself, but one critical question demands an answer first: Whence does objectivity takes its measure, against what "thing" does it measure itself? Helmut Kuhn has vividly explained how inadequate in this instance encapsulation in positivism is. *Homo faber* (man the maker), so he says, "understands how to make this or that, and what has just been made is 'good', in other words, it splendidly fulfills the particular purpose assigned to it. He produces transportation machines, and these machines are good, because they transport a maximum number of persons with a maximum speed over a maximum distance in space. Or he produces weapons, which again are good, because they are capable of annihilating a maximum number of persons . . . in a minimum of time. But the question of whether it is good for man to be transported in peace and to be killed in war as quickly as possible in the largest possible numbers—this question is beyond his competency."[13] The utter poverty of positivism is in plain view in these statements. What politics needs is a maximum of objective rationality, which seeks the greatest possible good without dogmatic fanaticism of any stamp whatsoever. But in order to be able to do that, reason needs a concept of the good, without which its objectivity becomes the plaything of special interest groups. Christian faith withstands the irrational divinization of politics; it wants politics to be reasonable, because it allows this world to be this world. It does not abolish reason; it challenges it and gives it stability by holding it to the standard of the eternal, the only thing that frees reason to be itself.

What should we do then? Before answering, let us look once again into the past and into the present; once again a

---

[13] H. Kuhn, *Der Staat* (Munich, 1967), 26f.

comment by Helmut Kuhn may be helpful here. "Over the centuries the peoples of Europe have striven with varying success after a political wisdom that is supposed to reconcile the common good with personal freedom, governance with equality, nationality with supranational regulation. Now, under the regime of its bloodthirsty future, all that effort seems to be in vain, as an attempt to varnish over the outrage of oppression."[14] What the Christian ought to do is this: beneath the standard of the eternal, to employ his reason in such a way that it can stand before the tribunal of the eternal. Faith is a task assigned to reason: to be itself. The only thing that it forbids is the irrationality that refuses to see things as they are and does not strive after the knowledge and realization of what is possible but rather spoils the possible with the impossible under the dominion of unrealistic ideals. The task of faith is: responsible reasonability; of course, responsibility (*Ver-antwort-ung*) exists only where there is an initial "word" (*Wort*) against which we are ultimately measured.

What, then, is faith good for? It is good for helping man to live, rejoice, and suffer. Indignation about suffering, which we are now taught and which pretends to be redemption, does not end the suffering but only makes it unbearable. Faith does not end suffering, either, but it makes people capable of carrying and sharing the burden. Man needs, not schoolmasters in indignation (he can learn that by himself), but, rather, teachers of transformation who uncover joy in the depth of suffering and open up true happiness where well-being leaves off. Anyone who reads Saint Francis' *Canticle of the Sun* and comes to understand this man, who in the collapse of his expectations was thrust physically and psychologically into the darkest night and yet was able to

---

[14] Kuhn, "Zukunftsmusik", 55.

praise God on account of his brother's death, knows how bright "heaven"—and heaven alone—can make the earth.

And so the whole topic comes around to the question that we repeat once more at the conclusion: What kind of salvation does faith offer? For what does it hope? Once again we must first say: It does not expect a politico-economic paradise—for faith, such an expectation is a farce staged by the Evil One, with which he deceives and enslaves man; we can all tell how true this is. From an earthly perspective, faith expects a world that will always be full of hardships; a world in which it will always be almost unbearably difficult to be a man; a world that never has a firm grasp on humanity but rather again and again requires men to become men. But because faith at the same time believes in and expects the world to come, it knows that it is nevertheless worthwhile and beautiful to toil in this world for justice and truth. Because it expects the next world, it can make man happy even now in the struggle for what he recognizes as lasting. The kingdom that "is not of this world", and it alone, makes even this world livable and worth living. Faith does not replace politics, but it creates something decisive without which politics, for all its safeguards and considerations, comes up empty: conscience, which makes a man trustworthy. Faith ensures that, despite appearances, there are always men whom one can trust and who themselves live by trust. In this respect, faith in the next world, of all things, is the prerequisite for being able to inhabit this world. Precisely because it is other-worldly, faith is also this-worldly, and where it loses its other-worldly character, not only does faith itself become an empty specter; then this whole world, too, becomes a haunted house where the spirits of cynicism and fanaticism go in and out. When the next world is declared an empty promise, then this world becomes desolate.

True consolation, however, embraces heaven and earth at the same time. Because it is true, it can afford the reason that takes things as they are: without the illusion of an earthly paradise, which stupefies reason and destroys freedom.

Conversing with Karl Rahner, S.J., at the reception hosted by the Catholic Academy to mark Rahner's seventy-fifth birthday; March 4, 1979 (Photograph: Academy Archive/Gerd Pfeiffer).

The Church

This text leads into the middle of the troubled time during the Second Vatican Council (1962–1965). It has its origin in a talk given at a conference held in Munich on February 9–10, 1963, on the theme of "The Second Vatican Council", which was an attempt, after the conclusion of the first session, to make an initial theological evaluation of the results in light of selected crucial topics. Besides Professor Ratzinger, at that time a professor of fundamental theology at the University of Bonn and a peritus (theological consultant) of the Archbishop of Cologne, Cardinal Joseph Frings, at the Council, other renowned scholars read papers, for instance, Auxiliary Bishop Walter Kampe (Limburg) and Professor Karl Rahner, S.J. (Innsbruck).

THE NATURE AND LIMITS
OF THE CHURCH

During the debate on the ecclesiological schema in December 1962, something happened that at first glance seems extremely odd. Twenty years previously, in the year 1943, the encyclical *Mystici corporis Christi* had appeared, which was well received by everyone, not least of all because it taught us to understand the Church as the Body of Christ. The new schema on the Church likewise built on this fundamental idea, but this is precisely what became the main starting point for criticism. Such a development is comprehensible only if one recognizes that the Church is a living thing that advances and grows in history; only if we recognize that, along with the Church herself, our understanding of the Church must be one that advances and grows. From this viewpoint, one can understand that what was progress in 1943 was not necessarily progress any more in 1962. At the same time, it becomes clear how difficult it is to arrive at a statement of the nature of the Church. Such a statement can be attempted only against the background of the historicity of this Church, and so, as a result, the initial task is that of understanding the intellectual movement in which both the event of the year 1943 as well as the one of 1962 have their place.

Translated by Michael J. Miller.

I. On the Question about the Nature of the Church

1. *The historical background of the encyclical* Mystici corporis

The movement out of which the 1943 encyclical grew goes far back to before the threshold of the Reformation and the new dogmatic definitions called into being by it. From around the thirteenth century, a profound transformation of the Body of Christ concept had taken place. The adjective "mystical" now acquired an intensified meaning; people talked about the "Mystical Body", which was supposed to signify much the same as body in the metaphorical sense, in other words, corporation. This idea of a "corporation" was also the reason why people now preferred to speak about the mystical body of the *Church* instead of the Mystical Body of Christ and thus declared the Church to be the corporation of Christians, which certainly had not been the old meaning of the Body of Christ image. Given this approach, arbitrary expansions of the image resulted almost automatically. John of Ragusa, for instance, differentiates regions of the head, of the hands, and of the feet in the body of the Church, by which he means the ecclesiastical authorities and dignitaries, the civil authorities, and finally the craftsmen and other trades.[1] Parallel to this developed the concept of the *res publica christiana*, of the *populus christianus*, that is, of Christendom as a reality in which political, cultural, and religious factors are jumbled together inseparably. In a series of liturgical texts dating from the fifteenth century, this

[1] Cf. B. Duda, *Joannis Stojković de Ragusio . . . doctrina de cognoscibilitate ecclesiae* (Rome, 1958), 104. See also p. 91, which says that in another passage John of Ragusa describes clerics as the soul and laymen as the body of the Church.

understanding of the Church as Christendom crystallized, most clearly perhaps in the prayer from the Mass against the heathens, which asks God to be mindful of Christians and to help them, "ut gentes paganorum, quae in sua feritate confidunt, dexterae tuae potentia conterantur" (that the heathen nations, which trust in their own fierceness, might be destroyed by the power of your right hand). Church is understood here almost in the sense of a Christian West that marks itself off from the heathens and asks for protection from them.[2] This understanding of the Church, which is defined in strongly juridical, indeed, political terms, becomes even more acute in the Reformation polemic, inasmuch as the Church is now accused of having degenerated into a "societas externarum rerum ac rituum" (association of external things and rites), of having changed into a worldly realm of ecclesiastical power, into a sort of papal state. The Reformation contrasts this process of externalization with its idea of the hidden quality of the Church and, in keeping with this approach, also gives a new twist to the Body of Christ concept, which becomes visible, for example, in the following sentence from the Defense of the Augsburg Confession:[3] "Although, therefore, hypocrites and wicked men are members of this true Church according to outward rites, titles and offices, yet when the Church is defined, it is necessary to define that which is called the body of Christ, and has fellowship not alone in outward signs, but has gifts

[2] Concerning this development, see the overview by E. Gilson (which of course sets out from other inquiries), *Les Métamorphoses de la cité de Dieu* (Louvain and Paris, 1952).

[3] Thus repeatedly in the Defense of the Augsburg Confession, in *Die Bekenntnisschriften der evangelisch-lutherischen Kirche*, 4th ed. (Göttingen, 1959), for instance: VII, 5, p. 234; VII, 10, p. 235; VII, 14, p. 236; and especially VII, 23f., pp. 239f. On the current Lutheran understanding of the Church, see, for example, E. Kinder, *Der evangelische Glaube und die Kirche* (Berlin, 1958).

in the heart, namely, the Holy Ghost and faith." [4] The term
"Body of Christ" is here reinterpreted as an expression for
the invisible inside of the Church; that it does in fact point in
this direction apparently struck Catholic theologians, too, as
something immediately obvious, and so this term necessarily
seemed to them to be not incorrect but dangerous nevertheless. In fact, even the Fathers of the First Vatican Council
repeatedly considered the designation of the Church as the
Body of Christ to be fraught with Protestant implications;
they still heard in it the protest against the visible hierarchical Church, in connection with which it had once played a
role. Only in this way is it comprehensible that from then
on the Body of Christ notion disappears from the Catholic
concept of Church; the post-Tridentine definitions of the
Church no longer mention this idea. Their point of departure lies in the idea of the people, which from the outset
accommodated an institutional understanding. Thus, for example, the *Roman Catechism* defines the Church as the faithful people scattered over the whole globe. [5] The well-known
definition by Bellarmine remained prominent for centuries:
The Church is the assembly of believers that is held together
by their profession of the same Christian faith and by the
fellowship of the same sacraments and is placed under the
care of their legitimate shepherds, especially the one Vicar
of Christ on earth, the Bishop of Rome. [6]

Not until around three hundred years later, in Catholic

[4] Defense, VII, 12, p. 236.

[5] Pars I, c. 1,02 (on the ninth article of the Creed): Communi vero
deinde sacrarum scripturarum consuetudine haec vox ad rem publicam
christianam . . . usurpata est; qui scilicet ad lucem veritatis et Dei noti-
tiam per fidem vocati sunt, ut rejectis ignorantiae et errorum tenebris,
Deum verum et vivum pie et sancte colant illique ex toto corde inserviant
atque . . . ut ait sanctus Augustinus, est populus fidelis per universum
orbem dispersus.

[6] *Disputationes de controversiis christianae fidei adversus hujus temporis hae-*

Romanticism, was the concept of the Mystical Body discovered once again in Catholic thought. The overtones of confessional controversies had died away, and in a new atmosphere of peace Catholic thought was more robustly willing to open itself to the intellectual impulses of the time and to help shape them. The discovery of the State and history by Hegel, on the one hand, and, on the other hand, the idea of the organism, which was characteristic of Romanticism as a whole, opened up entirely new possibilities for the teaching about the Church, which were promptly utilized. In 1825, Möhler published his study *Die Einheit in der Kirche* [*Unity in the Church*], which has remained a classic to this day, in which he constructed the idea of the Church in terms of the working of the Holy Spirit. In 1860, Pilgram's *Physiologie der Kirche* appeared, which already in its title manifests the author's organic thinking. In this way, however, two different lines of ecclesiological thinking now confronted each other: the old one derived from the *Roman Catechism* and Bellarmine, which thought about the Church in terms of the concept of the "People of God" and thus understood it primarily as a hierarchical institution,[7] while, on the other side, developed the new organic-mystical interpretation, which construed itself at the same time as a return to the Church Fathers. The ecclesiological schema that was presented to the Fathers of the First Vatican Coun-

---

reticos, 1586–1593. The definition is found in the fourth polemic ["On the Councils and the Church", bk. 3, sec. 2; quoted here with reference to the German edition by V. P. Gumposch (Augsburg, 1844), 228].

[7] Of course one should not overlook the fact that there is once again a considerable difference between the perspective of the *Catechismus Romanus* and that of Bellarmine: the *Roman Catechism* not incorrectly cites Augustine and still thinks to a great extent in terms of the Augustinian heritage, whereas Bellarmine's theology is conceived entirely in the controversy with the Reformers.

cil utilized the Body of Christ concept but by that very fact ran into major difficulties.[8] Ultimately, as you know, only the doctrine of the primacy was officially declared, which inadvertently resulted once again in a setback for the movement of ecclesiological thinking. The immediate task was to explain and defend this much contested doctrine, so that the problem of the primacy at first absorbed all the attention of ecclesiologists.

In the new theological breakthrough that followed the First World War, the promising approach of Romanticism then finally bore fruit. In the collapse of all previous security, Holy Mother Church was discovered anew; "the century of the Church"[9] seemed to have arrived. New editions of Möhler and Pilgram were printed. Scholars became enthusiastic about the writings of the Church Fathers, especially Augustine, and summed up their new appreciation and knowledge about the Church under her title of the Lord's Mystical Body.[10] Like a force of nature, this insight broke through centuries of ossification, and the fact that this new view of the Church received its ratification by the Church's Magisterium in the encyclical *Mystici corporis* was correctly

[8] The text is reprinted in Neuner-Dupuis, *The Christian Faith in the Doctrinal Documents of the Catholic Church*, 6th rev. ed. (New York: Alba House, 1996), 290–98; on the debate over the schema, see, for example, H. Rondet, *Vatican I* (Paris, 1962).

[9] *Das Jahrhundert der Kirche* is the title of a book by O. Dibelius (Berlin, 1928).

[10] A good survey of the ecclesiological work of these years can be found in C. Feckes, "Aus dem Ringen um das Kirchenbild", *Theologie der Zeit*, 2nd series (Vienna, 1936), 154–62. See also Stephan Jaki, *Les Tendences nouvelles de l'ecclésiologie* (Rome, 1957); especially instructive is Y. Congar, "Dogme christologique et ecclésiologie", in *Chalkedon III*, ed. H. Bacht and A. Grillmeier (Würzburg, 1954), 239–68. There is an extensive bibliography in M. Schmaus, *Katholische Dogmatik*, 5th ed., vol. 3, pt. 1 (1958), 842–88.

perceived as a major event, for it was possible to see this as a victory over the one-sided hierarchical understanding of the Church and, at the same time, as an official affirmation of everything new that had sprung up in theology since Möhler.

Of course, when the encyclical appeared, the development in actuality had already advanced a step farther and was temporarily hindered in its development only by the war. But the outline of what must come was already being clearly drawn. What had happened between the world wars was a beginning, but the matter could not rest there. Theologians had heaped upon the image of the Mystical Body all the glories of the supernatural and thereby created an extremely unrealistic concept, which alongside the all-too-human reality of the Church must have seemed like a dream; the Romantic approach could overlook this for a moment but could not disguise it indefinitely. In fact, theologians had been aware of the problem, but they had taken care of it by subdividing ecclesiology. The previous institutional ecclesiology was not simply to be dismantled but was to be left standing, unchanged, as an apologetic teaching about the Church. Alongside it, however, they now wanted to set up a second, dogmatic teaching about the Church, which would then deal with the mystical glory of her interior. But who could forget for long that the mystical glory remains meaningless, empty talk if the concrete Church presents herself to us as something so completely different? In the long run, there was no getting around the fact that the interior appears and is real only in the exterior and that the exterior is tolerable only if it signifies inseparably the self-bestowal of the interior. For this reason, the juxtaposition of two kinds of ecclesiology could not be a solution, since the real problem is precisely the meshing of glory and lowliness.

At around the same time appeared critical studies by

Oswald Holzer,[11] Ludwig Deimel,[12] Johannes Beumer,[13] Erich Przywara,[14] and especially by Mannes Dominikus Koster [1940].[15] In different ways, they all made one thing clear: the fact that Church cannot be construed in terms of a mystical idea, because in that way one cannot deal with her visible character. Similarly it was now emphasized that biblical thought does not mean the particular person individualistically, who then would be united "mystically", in a hidden way, with the grace of the Lord; instead, starting from the covenant with God, it looks first to the whole and then to the individual as part of the whole. The contemporaneous studies by Henri de Lubac went into even greater depth on account of their astonishing historical erudition; moreover, he developed the new approach in terms of patristic tradition.[16]

In the critical studies just mentioned, there was again talk, above all, of the People of God as the more comprehensive and more realistic concept; the "mysticism" of the *corpus* concept was again viewed rather suspiciously as incapable of doing justice to the true realities—and this by theologians whom one could not simply write off as heirs to Bellarmine

[11] "Christus in uns", a critique of the recent literature on the Mystical Body of Christ, in *Wissenschaft und Weisheit* 8 (1941): 24f.; 64–70; 93–105; 130–36.

[12] *Leib Christi* (Freiburg, 1940).

[13] "Apologetik oder Dogmatik der Kirche" in *Theologie und Glaube* 31 (1939): 379–91.

[14] "*Corpus Christi Mysticum:* Eine Bilanz", *Zeitschrift für Aszese und Mystik* 15 (1940): 197–215.

[15] *Ekklesiologie im Werden.*

[16] Especially *Catholicism*, trans. Lancelot C. Sheppard and Elizabeth Englund (San Francisco: Ignatius Press, 1988); *Corpus mysticum*, 2nd ed. (Paris, 1949). Concerning the "Eucharistic concept of the Church" that was inaugurated thereby, see also especially J. Hamer, *L'Église est une communion* (Paris, 1962), as well as the corresponding pages in P. Evdokimov, *L'Orthodoxie* (Neuchâtel and Paris, 1960), which at the same time show the ecumenical importance of these findings.

and a one-sided anti-Reformation theology but, rather, who feared that the Body of Christ idea could lead to a false glorification of the Church of the Cross and, therefore, were concerned that the earthly lowliness of the pilgrim Church should not be covered over with the golden gleam of a false halo. Furthermore, they were anxious that the biblical picture, which looks to the individual in terms of the covenant, not become submerged in modern thinking about organisms or in an individualistic mysticism. "People of God" and "Body of Christ" thus were and are once again two contrasting approaches to the concept of Church. This situation, which in 1943 was still only coming about, is fully developed today; it defined the discussion of the Council.

2. *The present-day status of the discussion*

What should we say about this dilemma? The right path, it seems to me, has been marked out by the works of de Lubac, which draw upon a wealth of sources. For the answer cannot come from any passionately defended speculative theories about the nature of the Church; nor can it come from an endless interpretation of magisterial documents of the Church, which, indeed, are supposed, not to replace advancing theological research, but, rather, to formulate what is authentic in the work that has already been done. The solution can come only from a thorough, precise reflection on Scripture and on tradition as a whole in light of Scripture. It goes without saying that something like that cannot be attempted within the framework of such a limited lecture; we can only try to sketch with the utmost conciseness a few baselines from the studies already completed.

The simplest and least dubious way of probing the New Testament understanding of Church could be to start simply from the name that the first community of believers

gave itself, which was able to prevail over all other desig-
nations because it corresponded best to the historical self-
understanding of the nascent Church: ἐκκλησία. This word
contains initially a twofold historical reminiscence. It recalls
the popular assembly of Greece, in which the *polis* fulfilled
its proper nature as a state. Secondly, it recalls the popular
assembly of Israel, in which a people likewise fulfilled itself
as a people; it differed from the popular assembly in Greece,
however, in that here not only men met, but also women
and children. This was because in this meeting, unlike in
the Greek assembly, it was a matter, not of deciding what
to do, but, rather, of hearing and thereby of accepting what
God had decided. Thus the assembly of the listening people
around Sinai appeared as the primordial image of the Israelite
popular assembly in general: Israel's self-actualization comes
to pass in its common listening to the word of God, from
which this people receives its existence as a people. In calling itself *ekklesia*, the congregation of those who believe in
Christ now transfers this image to itself. It interprets itself
as the assembly of the definitive Israel, in which God calls
his people together from all the ends of the earth.[17]

In its concrete linguistic usage, early Christianity subdi-
vides the word *ekklesia* into a threefold spectrum of meaning:
it designates the worshipping assembly,[18] the local community,[19] and the universal Church.[20] These three basic meanings overlap in such a way that the particular local commu-

---

[17] On this subject, see especially O. Linton, "Ekklesia" in *RAC* 4:905–
21, esp. 905–9.

[18] For example, 1 Cor 11:18, 14:19, 28, 34, 35.

[19] For example, 1 Cor 1:2; 16:1 et passim.

[20] For example, 1 Cor 15:9, Gal 1:13, Phil 3:6 et passim. On this whole
subject, see the analysis by A. Wikenhauser, *Die Kirche als der mystische
Leib Christi nach dem Apostel Paulus* (Münster, 1940), 4–21, which is still
worthwhile, and above all the summary presentation by R. Schnackenburg, *Die Kirche im Neuen Testament* (Freiburg, 1961). The following

nity appears as the representation of the one overall reality Church, of this one, indivisible, eschatological idea of God, and then again the worshipping assembly is considered to be the concrete realization of the ecclesial nature of the individual Church. Consequently, we have the following connection among the three levels of meaning: there is the one entity of the *ekklesia*, the People of God, which God gathers for himself in this world. This one Church of God exists concretely in the various individual local communities and in turn realizes herself there in the worshipping assembly. To put it more clearly: just as the people Israel, while scattered throughout the earth, nevertheless became and remained one through the Temple and actualized its unity every year in the Passover celebration in and around the Temple, so too the geographically scattered communities of Christian believers became one because of the new temple, namely, the Body of the Lord. They are one as *ekklesia*, that is, as God's worshipping assembly, in which they eat the one bread that makes them one Body, in which they bear witness to the one Word through which they are of one mind and spirit. They no longer need either the geographically one Temple or the unity of lineage and blood because they have a deeper unity: the unity of the one bread, through which the Lord unites them with one another and with himself; the unity of the one Word in which the one Spirit of the Lord testifies to himself in them. Although we can say, then, that the word *ekklesia* takes up the idea of Israel, the people called by God, and accordingly means the same as "People of God", this people is nevertheless specified more precisely by the fact that it lives on the Body of Christ and the Word of Christ and in this way becomes the Body of Christ itself.

---

discussion follows closely my exposition of the subject in the article "Kirche", in *LThK* 6:172–83.

On this basis, one could very concisely define Church as *People of God resulting from the Body of Christ*. She has in common with the people of the Old Covenant the fact that she is the People of God; the fact that she is so in the Body of Christ is, in a manner of speaking, her *differentia specifica* as a new people, and this designates her particular way of existing and being one. This statement in turn refers back to the foundation that Jesus himself laid: he called the Twelve as the image of Israel, the *People* of God; he definitively founded the Church by celebrating the *Last Supper* with the Twelve, and thus he gave them the new thing that distinguished them from the old Israel. The Pauline description of the Church as the Body of Christ is basically something new only in its formulation; in fact, it is simply the explanation of this state of affairs established by the Lord himself: the fact that the new people receives its specific reality from the Lord's Supper.

The Church is Body of Christ because she receives the Body of the Lord in the Lord's Supper and lives on this core. One immediate consequence of this statement, to which our reflections thus far have led us, is that "Body of Christ" is not a concept of the mystical order for the invisible, mysterious interior of the Church (as it had been misunderstood since the Romantic period, or actually since the Reformation), but, rather, her *concretissimum* (most concrete feature), which of course at the same time inseparably carries within it the inmost depth of her life: the celebration of the Lord's Supper. The expression *corpus Christi* depicts the Church as the community of those who celebrate the Lord's Supper together; it is a term that thoroughly expresses the visibility of the Church and, of course, inseparably from that, her hidden foundation. And so this puts into words exactly what we are looking for: the inseparability of outside and inside, the being of the Church as *sacramentum Dei* (the sacrament of God) in this world. The idea of Holy Orders, of ministry as service to the Body and Word of the Lord, is also present in this expression; indeed, the meaning of ecclesial ministry from the primacy to the simplest services rendered can be understood correctly only in terms of this center. And finally: although the Church appears here as altogether visible, at the same time, the peculiar manner of this visibility becomes evident, namely, the fact that this is the visibility of a window, whose nature is to refer beyond itself.

Based on such insights, the Fathers did not hesitate to characterize the Church as the true Body of the Lord (*corpus verum*), whereas at least from time to time the Eucharist was called *corpus mysticum* (*mysticum = sacramentale*).[21] A fundamental feature of linguistic usage well into the twelfth century was the inseparable intertwining of the eucharistic and the ecclesial Body, the knowledge that the Church is built up by and from the Eucharist and that the Church, on the other hand, cannot be understood and defined without the Eucharist. Only in the twelfth century does a change come about in the use of the word *mysticum*, which now is applied no longer to the Eucharist but, instead, to the Church. At the same time, we find already behind this a shift in the meaning of the word, which is no longer the expression of the sacramental order but rather an indication of an allegory. With that we have arrived at our starting point: the concept of Body slips into the juridical sphere.[22] At this juncture,

[21] For the details, see De Lubac, *Corpus mysticum*, esp. 89–122. My article "Leib Christi", in *LThK* 2:910ff., offers a short survey of the individual stages of the development. At least one of the most characteristic texts for the oscillation between the eucharistic and the ecclesiological Body concepts should be mentioned here: "Corpus Christi manducare nihil aliud est quam corpus Christi effici" (To eat the Body of Christ is nothing other than to be made the body of Christ), William of Saint Thierry, *Liber de natura et dignitate amoris* 13, 38 PL 184:403.

[22] The prerequisite for it, of course, was not created until the twelfth

we must not forget to mention that in Paul's writings and in those of the Fathers the expression *corpus Christi mysticum* does not exist; instead, the Church is simply called "Body of Christ" (without an adjective).

In retrospect, one can say that history has distanced itself from the original Body of Christ concept and has modified it decisively twice. The real problem with the Body of Christ doctrine lies in these historical overlays. Looking back, we can now ascertain three historical rings:

1. the *biblical-patristic* concept: Church as the People of God, which is gathered up into the Body of Christ in the celebration of the Eucharist. One could speak of a *sacramental-ecclesiological understanding*; the following equation is true: *ecclesia = communio = Corpus Christi*;

2. alongside this there is the *medieval* concept: theologians speak about a *corpus ecclesiae mysticum*; Church appears as a corporation of Christ (and not as the "Body" of Christ!). One could speak of a *corporate-juridical understanding of the Body*;

3. the modern era develops the *Romantic* concept: *corpus Christi mysticum* = the mysterious mystical organism of Christ; the word "mystical" is derived from mysticism. We are confronted with the *organological-mystical understanding*.

When the first concept is taken as the starting point, there is no antithesis at all to the People of God concept. "People of God" is taken up into "Body of Christ" as the Old Testament into the New. In this case, there is no dilemma, either, about whether the Church is an "institution or a form of mysticism". In the second and the third and in any other case, however, the result is a hopeless constriction of the various aspects of ecclesial reality. Reinstating the first con-

---

century, and its appearance occurs in the thirteenth and fourteenth centuries.

cept, on the other hand, means carrying out a real *reformatio*: overcoming the weight of history and purifying the present in terms of the origin—herein lies the great opportunity and the task of the Council.

II. The Question of Membership in the Church

1. *Body of Christ and Roman Catholic Church*

Given these insights, there is now a further problem to elucidate, which leads from the question about the nature of the Church to the one about her limits. The encyclical *Mystici corporis* had caused a sensation by proposing the equation *corpus Christi mysticum* = Roman Catholic Church, which naturally reoccurred in the conciliar schema on the Church. Upon publication of the encyclical, this rigorous equation had already caused several difficulties for its commentators;[23] in the debates of the Council, it elicited protests from ecumenically minded bishops.

What are we to say about that? The illumination of the historical dimensions of the Body of Christ concept might provide the key. If one interprets the concept in the patristic manner along the lines of the equation Church = *communio*, and if it therefore expresses the sacramental communion of those who communicate with one another in the Body of Christ, then the identification with the concrete *communio eucharistica* is in principle justified. Of course this identification cannot be expressed without provisos, because a certain association with the *communio* is characteristic of all

[23] Cf. especially A. Mitterer, *Geheimnisvoller Leib Christi nach Sankt Thomas von Aquin und nach Papst Pius XII* (Vienna, 1950); J. Beumer, "Die Identität des Mystischen Leibes Christi und der katholischen Kirche", *ThGl* 44 (1954): 321–38.

baptized persons—an association that unequivocally distinguishes them from the situation of the non-baptized. We will have to speak about that again in a moment. If one understands the concept along medieval lines institutionally and hierarchically, then the equation is unambiguous. Finally, if one understands it along the lines of the modern notion of the *corpus mysticum*, the identification is meaningless and false, because in the hidden order of grace that is thereby suggested such a restriction quite obviously can have no place.

The problem with the equation articulated in the encyclical as well as in the conciliar schema is that in those documents the *Corpus Christi* concept is imprecise and undefined and contains elements from all three levels just mentioned. We should add that the enduring formula *corpus Christi mysticum*, which is neither Pauline nor patristic and is unusual for the Middle Ages as well, refers primarily to the intellectual heritage of the Romantic ecclesiology of the nineteenth and twentieth century and consequently makes the identification with the Roman Church seem hardly tolerable. The hidden mystery of Christ's spiritual operation, as we said, cannot be confined to the limits of the visible Church.[24] In these facts lies the legitimate approach to the criticism that has now become quite vocal.

2. Membership in the Church

Thus we are confronted with the question: "Who belongs to the *communio* of the Church?"—in other words, with the problem of Church membership.[25] On this subject there

[24] Cf. especially Y. Congar, "Ecclesia ab Abel", in *Abhandlungen über Theologie und Kirche: Festschrift für Karl Adam* (Düsseldorf, 1952), 79–108, and the critical response to it in F. Malmberg, *Ein Leib—Ein Geist* (Freiburg, 1960), 89–102.

[25] On this question, see K. Mörsdorf and K. Rahner, "Kirchenglied-

have long been two contrasting traditions within Catholic theology. First, there is a more canonical strand of tradition that is crystallized in canon 87 of the [1917] CIC, which says that a man becomes a "person in the Church" through baptism. Besides this, there is a dogmatic-apologetic line of tradition that was eventually and emphatically formulated in the 1943 encyclical and likewise had entered into the new schema on the Church. According to this tradition, only someone who is united with the Church in his profession of faith, reception of the sacraments, and subordination to the hierarchy (including the pope) and is not excommunicated is a member of the Church. In contrast to the canonical strand of tradition, which teaches that every baptized individual should be regarded as a member of the Church, the question thereby arises about the Christian status of non-Catholic Christians. This problem is dealt with here by means of the distinction *reapse-voto*, which states that Catholics are "really" members of the Church, while the others could be "by desire" (*voto*). Three things weigh against such a solution: (1) It involves a fictitious psychology, inasmuch as it imputes to our separated brethren a wish that they consciously and expressly deny. (2) It in fact includes a comparison of non-Catholic Christians with pagans with regard to Church membership, because belonging to the Church by desire can be ascribed just as well to the latter. (3) The starting point of this attempt at a solution remains completely within the subjective realm; the salvation of non-Catholics is in practice reduced exclusively to the subjective factor of a desire, which, furthermore, cannot even be observed as a conscious phenomenon.

Behind this duality of traditions there is at a deeper level a

---

schaft", in *LThK* 6:221–25 with bibliography; see also my remarks in ibid., 179f., and *RGG* 5:664.

twofold sacramental point of departure: canon law thinks in terms of baptism as the sacrament of becoming a Christian; everything Christian, however, has to do with the Church. There is no such thing as a merely individual Christianity; instead, being Christian always means belonging to the whole Christ and, thus, to the Church. But since there is only one Church, everyone who is a Christian must, in one form or another, be a member of the one Church.

The second tradition, on the other hand, is plainly connected with the equation Church = *communio*, which says that the essential content of being a Christian is communicating in the Body of the Lord. But if Church is communion-fellowship, then only someone who communicates [that is, receives communion] is in the Church. This results automatically in the restriction to the membership criteria mentioned previously. Nevertheless, even in this case it is still true that those who are "excommunicated" have a different relation to the Church than the non-baptized. Through baptism they became in principle members who belong to the communion-fellowship, even though as a matter of fact they have taken a stand outside the unity of the *communio*. Overlooking this is no doubt the mistake that must be noted in relation to the theses of the second line of tradition. The Church cannot and must not acquiesce in leaving those separated from her communion to their own devices, much less in disregarding the fact that they are Christians. The fact that the multitude of those who are not in communion with her is larger today than the inner circle of communicants is her sorrow, the deep wound in the Body of the Lord, which she must suffer as her own wound. In both cases, therefore, the facts remain: there are different forms of membership in the Church, but every baptized person participates in the Church. The question of the terminology in which one wants to express this state of affairs is in comparison secondary. Above all, if the proponents of what we have called the dogmatic strand of tradition say that the concept of an imperfect member is self-contradictory, a misplaced metaphor, one can readily grant them their point.[26] In fact, it is not necessary at all to elaborate on the various ways of belonging to the Church by using the image of the member specifically. The one crucial thing is that the matter under discussion here be expressed, that the Christian status of our separated brethren be recognized and at the same time that the wound of the Church caused by their separation not be ignored.

If we look at things this way, then it automatically follows that the all-too-hasty amalgamation of the question of membership with the question of salvation is dissolved. It can only be detrimental to the objectivity of the inquiry if the question about Church membership is always immediately burdened with the question about the path to salvation of the respective groups. It must first be answered in itself, in terms of the objective criteria resulting from the concept of Church. Only in the second place can one then pose the question of how the groups of people so defined participate in the one salvation of Jesus Christ, which is present in the Church. The radius of this second question of course reaches farther; not only Christians but all mankind must be included in it.

3. Church and the world's salvation

Now as for this problem of the salvation of the many, surely it cannot be up to the Council to provide an elaborate theory

[26] See the presentation, once again summarizing this position, by H. Schauf, "Zur Frage der Kirchengliedschaft", *Theol. Revue* 58 (1962): 217-24.

of it. The new view of man and of the world that the findings of the last few centuries have set before us has raised
new questions in this regard, brought new facts into our
field of vision, and, thus, established completely new starting points for the discussion.[27] Here it will be necessary
to keep grappling carefully and seriously in order to reconcile what is apparently contradictory. Ultimately the Council will be able to state only the factual findings that have
already been established, without attempting a synthesis, in
other words, it will have to set forth the twofold state of
affairs, on the one hand, that all salvation is ecclesially struc-
tured and ecclesially mediated and, on the other hand, that
this salvation is accessible to all men, whenever and wherever they live.

If in the foregoing remarks it has become clear that the
question about Church membership and the question about
salvation are closely interdependent yet not identical, then
this recognition will also make possible a new view of the
missionary problem. No doubt missionary work is connected with salvation and is performed with a view to the
salvation of mankind. Nevertheless, that is not the sole or
perhaps not even the first and real reason for missionary
work.[28] We no longer share the opinion of Francis Xavier
that without the missions mankind, one and all, would go
to hell. Besides and perhaps even prior to its direct connection with salvation, the reason for missionary work is

---

[27] On this whole question, see the excellent presentation by Y. Congar, *The Wide World My Parish: Salvation and Its Problems*, trans. Donald
Attwater (Baltimore: Helicon Press, 1961).

[28] On the current status of the question about the theology of the missions, see especially M. J. Le Guillou, *Mission et unité: Les Exigences de la
communion* (Paris, 1960); Y. de Montcheuil, *Kirche und Wagnis des Glaubens*
(Freiburg, 1957), esp. 186–202; T. Ohm, *Machet zu Jüngern alle Völker*
(Freiburg, 1962); G. F. Vicedom, *Missio Dei* (Munich, 1958).

that in this way the Church carries out her own inner dynamic, her openness to everyone, by symbolically expressing the hospitality of God, who has invited all men to be guests at the wedding feast of his Son. That divine abundance, which is characteristic of God's work in creation and salvation history, is expressed in missionary work, also, in which the Church opens herself and imitates and participates in the overflowing of divine love outward. Furthermore, missionary work must take place so that history is brought to its destination and the torn body of mankind is led back to unity. The essence of sin is separation into individual selfishness. Sin is a mystery of separation and strife, through which mankind is split up into the selfishness of the many, each of whom knows and understands only himself. Its mysterious symbol is Babel, the place of the confusion of tongues, where selfishness broke down the bridges of understanding. The essence of the Christ event, in contrast, is unification, the bringing back together of the scattered members of mankind into one body. Its symbol is the Pentecost event, the miracle of understanding that creates love and brings what was separated into unity. In missionary work, the Church thus actualizes the real nature of salvation history, the mystery of unification. Missionary work occurs so as to perfect the miracle of Pentecost, to heal the strife that splits up the body of mankind, and to lead it out of Babel into the pentecostal reality. Thus what the Church is becomes completely visible only in the missions: service to the mystery of the unification that Christ intended to bring about in his crucified Body.[29]

---

[29] These ideas are developed extensively in terms of patristic theology in J. Ratzinger, "Die Vision der Väter von der Einheit der Völker", *Der katholische Gedanke* 19 (1963): 1–9.

*An audience of almost a thousand responded in Munich on June 4,
1970, to an invitation from the Catholic Academy in Bavaria to
an evening lecture by Professor Joseph Ratzinger, then Ordinarius
for Dogmatics at the University of Regensburg. Evidently the topic,
"Why I Am Still in the Church Today", had squarely addressed a
problem that occupied the minds of many people. The second speech
for the defense in the series "Christian Life and Church" was given
on June 11, 1970, with a similarly great response, by the theologian
Dr. Hans Urs von Balthasar from Basel (Switzerland) with the title "Why I Am Still a Christian Today".*

WHY I AM STILL IN THE CHURCH[1]

Today there are many and conflicting reasons not to be in the Church any more. The people who feel driven today to turn their backs on the Church are not only the ones who have become alienated from the Church's faith or who regard the Church as too old-fashioned, too medieval, too hostile to the world and life, but also those who loved the historical form of the Church, her worship, her timelessness, and the reflection of the eternal in her. It seems to them that the Church is in the process of betraying what is most characteristic of her, that she is selling herself to current fashion and thus losing her soul: they are disappointed like a lover who has to experience the betrayal of a great love and must seriously consider turning his back on her.

Conversely, however, there are also quite conflicting reasons to stay in the Church: the ones who remain are not only those who steadfastly adhere to their faith in her mission or those who are unwilling to sever their ties to a dear old habit (even though they make little use of that habit).

Translated by Michael J. Miller.

[1] Given the parameters of a lecture and the special nature of the theme assigned to me, it goes without saying that it was not possible to attempt a comprehensive presentation of the objective reasons for being in the Church. I had to be content with fitting together, as though in a mosaic, a few remarks about a decision that is ultimately my own personal responsibility, which nonetheless can perhaps make evident in their own way something of an objective law.

Also remaining in the Church today, quite emphatically, are those who reject her entire historical character and passionately fight against the meaning that her officials try to give to her or uphold. Although they want to do away with what the Church was and is, they are determined not to be ousted, so that they can make of her what, in their opinion, she is supposed to become.

Preliminary Reflection on the Situation of the Church

All this, however, produces a veritable Tower of Babel within the Church: not only are the reasons pro and con mixed up in the strangest ways, but now it hardly seems possible to reach any agreement. Above all, mistrust is on parade, because being in the Church has lost its clear meaning and in the resulting ambiguity no one dares to trust the other's honesty. Romano Guardini's hopeful assessment, written in 1921, seems to have turned into its opposite. "A momentous process has begun: the Church is awakening in souls." Today, it seems that the saying should read the other way around: indeed, a momentous process is taking place —the Church is being extinguished in souls and is collapsing in communities. In the midst of a world that is striving for unity, the Church is crumbling into nationalistic resentment, the denunciation of anything foreign and the glorification of what is one's own. Between the managers of worldliness and the reactionaries who cling all too much to externals and to what merely has been, between a disregard for tradition and positivistic building upon the letter of the law, there seems to be no middle ground—public opinion implacably assigns each to his place; it needs clear labels and cannot be bothered about nuances: Anyone who is not for progress is against it; one has to be either a conservative or a progressive. Of course the reality, thank God, is different: quietly and almost voicelessly, between those extremes there are, even today, simple believers, who even in this hour of confusion carry out the real task of the Church: worship and the patience of everyday life, nourished by the Word of God. But they do not fit into the desired picture, and so they remain for the most part silent—this true Church, while not invisible, is nevertheless hidden deep beneath the human additives.

This gives us a preliminary hint about the background for the question that arises today: Why do I still stay in the Church? If we are to answer it meaningfully, we must first analyze in greater depth this background, which because of that little word "today" is directly concerned with our topic, and we must now go beyond identifying the situation to inquire into the reasons for it.

How could this remarkable Tower of Babel situation come about just when we were hoping to have a new Pentecost? How was it possible that at the very moment when the Council seemed to have gathered in the mature harvest from the awakening of the last decades, the result was suddenly a frightening emptiness instead of a wealth of fulfillment? How could it happen that this great new movement aimed at unity should produce disintegration? I would like to try, first, to answer with a comparison, which at the same time can reveal the task before us and, thereby, suggest the reasons that, despite all that is negative, continue to make an affirmative possible. It seems that in our efforts to understand the Church—which finally at the Council became an active struggle over her, a concrete project of working on the Church—we got so close to this same Church that now we no longer manage to perceive the whole. We can no longer see the city for the houses, the forest for the trees. This situation, into which science has so often led us with regard to reality, seems to have come about now with respect to the Church as well. We see the particular detail with such excessive precision that it becomes impossible for us to perceive the whole. And just as in science, so too here: the gain in exactitude means a loss of truth. However indisputably correct everything is that the microscope shows us when we look at a piece of a tree under it, it can still, at the same time, conceal the truth if it causes us to forget that the particular detail is not just the particular but has its existence within the whole, which cannot be put under the microscope and yet is true, truer than the isolated detail.

Let us say things now without metaphor. The contemporary perspective has further modified our view of the Church: in practice, we see the Church now exclusively under the aspect of feasibility, what we can make out of her. The intensive effort for reform in the Church finally caused everything else to be forgotten; to us today she is only a structure that we can change, which confronts us with the question of what we ought to change so as to make her "more efficient" for whatever purposes the individual may have in mind. In the popular mind-set, the idea of reform has to a great extent degenerated into this way of framing the question and thus has been robbed of its essence. For reform, in the original sense, is a spiritual process, quite closely related to conversion and in this sense part of the core of Christianity: only through conversion does one become a Christian; this is true for the individual throughout his lifetime, and this is true for the Church throughout all of history. She, too, as Church, lives on the fact that she is converted again and again to the Lord and turns away from her stubborn insistence on what is her own, on mere habit, which, although comforting, can so easily be contrary to the truth. But when reform is separated from this context, from the drudgery of conversion, and salvation is now expected solely from change in other people, from ever new forms and ever new adaptations to the age, then many useful things may still happen, but overall it becomes a caricature of itself. Strictly speaking, such reform can affect only the unimportant, secondary things in the Church; no wonder the Church herself in the end appears to be of secondary importance! If we reflect on that, then we also understand the paradox that seems to have resulted from present-day efforts of renewal: the effort to loosen up rigid structures, to correct forms of ecclesiastical ministry that date back to the Middle Ages or, even more, to the era of absolutism, and to free the Church from such accretions for the sake of a simpler service in the spirit of the Gospel—this effort has in fact led to an overemphasis on the official element in the Church that is almost unprecedented in history. Granted, the institutions and offices in the Church are being criticized more radically today than ever before, but they are also absorbing our attention more exclusively than they did formerly: quite a few people suppose that the Church today consists of those things alone. The question about the Church is then exhausted in the fight over her institutions; people do not want such an elaborate apparatus to go unused, yet they find it largely impractical for the new purposes that are assigned to it.

Behind this another point, the crucial one, becomes visible: the crisis of faith, which is the actual nucleus of the process. With regard to her sociological radius, the Church still extends far beyond the circle of actual believers, and

through this institutionalized untruth she has become profoundly alienated from her true nature. The heavy publicity
surrounding the Council and the apparent possibility of a
rapprochement between belief and unbelief (which the news
coverage almost inevitably feigned) radicalized this alienation to the extreme: the applause for the Council came
partly from those who had no intention whatsoever of becoming believers themselves, as Christian tradition understands it, but rather greeted the "progress" that the Church
was making toward their own stance as a corroboration of
their way. At the same time, of course, the faith was in an exciting state of ferment within the Church, too. The problem
of historical mediation causes the old Creed to enter into
an indistinct twilight in which the outlines of things blur;
the claims of the natural sciences, and still more of what is
considered to be the modern world view, do their part to ag-
gravate this process. The boundaries between interpretation
and denial become increasingly unrecognizable, right at the
heart of the matter: What does "risen again from the dead"
really mean? Who is believing, who is interpreting, who is
denying? And in all the debate about the limits of interpretation, the face of God is noticeably disappearing. "The death
of God" is a very real process, which today extends deep into
the interior of the Church. God is dying in Christendom, so
it seems. For when resurrection becomes an experience of
a commission perceived in outmoded imagery, then God is
not at work. Is he at work at all? That is the question that immediately follows. But who wants to be so reactionary as to
insist on a realistic "he is risen"? Thus what one person necessarily considers unbelief is progress to another, and what
was hitherto unthinkable becomes normal: that men who
long ago abandoned the Church's Creed should in good conscience regard themselves as the truly progressive Christians.

For them, however, the only standard by which to measure the Church is the expediency with which she functions; of course the question remains as to what is expedient and for what purpose the whole thing is actually supposed to function. For social criticism, for developmental aid, for revolution? Or for community celebrations? In any case, one must start over from the ground up, because the Church was not originally made for all that, and besides, in her present form she is probably not really capable of functioning like that, either. So the uneasiness among believers and unbelievers increases. The property right that unbelief has acquired in the Church makes the situation seem increasingly intolerable to both groups; above all, through these developments, the reform program has tragically drifted into an odd ambiguity for which many people no longer see any solution.

Now naturally one can say: But that is not the whole situation that we are facing. Indeed, there have also been so many positive developments in recent years that simply cannot be ignored—the new accessibility of the liturgy, the heightened awareness of social problems, better understanding among separated Christians, the dismantling of many fears that had sprung from a false faith in the letter of the law, and much more. That is true and it should not be belittled. But it is not characteristic of the "prevailing weather system" in the Church today (if I may put it that way). On the contrary, all this, too, has meanwhile been drawn into the twilight that has resulted from the blurring of the boundaries between belief and unbelief. Only initially did the result of this blurring seem to be liberating. Today it is clear that, despite all the existing signs of hope, this process has produced, not a modern Church, but one that is deeply divided and doubtful all around. Let us put it quite bluntly: The First Vatican Council had described the Church as "signum levatum in nationes" (a signal flag raised for the nations), as the great eschatological banner visible from afar that summons and unites mankind. She is (the 1870 Council said) that "ensign" or standard for which Isaiah hoped (11:12), visible from afar, which everyone can recognize and which unambiguously shows the way to all: with her miraculous propagation, her sublime sanctity, her fruitfulness in every good work, and her unshakable stability, she is the real miracle of Christianity, its constant authentication in the sight of history, replacing all other signs and wonders.[2] Today all this seems to have turned into the opposite: not marvelous propagation, but a parochial, stagnant club that was incapable of surpassing in earnest the limits of the European or the medieval mind; not sublime sanctity, but, rather, a compendium of all human offenses, defiled and humiliated by a history that has not missed a single scandal, from the burning of heretics to witch hunts, from the persecution of Jews and the enslavement of consciences to self-dogmatization and resistance to scientific evidence, so that anyone who belongs to this history can only cover his head in shame; and finally, not stability, but, rather, being swept along by all the currents of history, by colonialism and nationalism, and now in the process of coming to terms with Marxism and, if possible, largely identifying herself with it. . . . Thus the Church appears to be, not a sign summoning us to faith, but, rather, the chief obstacle to accepting it.

If there is to be a true theology of the Church now, it seems that it can only consist of taking away her theological attributes and regarding and discussing her as something purely political. The Church herself seems to be no longer a reality of the faith but a quite accidental, even if perhaps

[2] Denzinger-Schönmetzer, *Enchiridion Symbolorum*, 32nd ed. (Freiburg, 1963), nos. 3013f.

indispensable, organization of believers, which ought to be restructured as quickly as possible according to the latest findings of sociology. Trust is good, but verification is better—after all the disappointments, this is now the slogan with regard to ecclesial office. The sacramental principle is no longer intelligible; democratic checks and balances seem now to be the only reliable alternative:[3] even the Holy Spirit, after all, is much too intangible. Anyone who is not afraid to look at the past knows, of course, that the humiliations of history were based precisely on following this path: man managed to seize power and considered his accomplishments to be the only real thing.

An Image for the Nature of the Church

A Church that is viewed only in political terms, contrary to her entire history and her distinctive nature, makes no sense, and a merely political decision to remain in the Church is dishonest, even if it chants the slogan of honesty. But then, given the present situation, how can one justify staying in the Church? To put it differently: The decision in favor of the Church must be a spiritual decision, if it is to have any meaning—but how can such a spiritual decision be justified? Once again I would like to give a preliminary answer in a comparison, while referring back to the statement offered initially to describe the situation. We had said that in tampering with the Church we have come so close to her that our perception of the whole is gone. We can enlarge on this

---

[3] There may be some justification for such a demand, and to a large extent it may be quite compatible with the sacramentally defined form of Church leadership; this point is developed, with the necessary distinctions, in J. Ratzinger and H. Maier, *Demokratie in der Kirche* (Limburg, 1970).

thought by applying an image that the Church Fathers found
in their symbolic meditation on the Church and the world.
They explained that in the arrangement of the cosmos, the
moon is an image for what the Church is in the arrangement of salvation in the spiritual-intellectual universe. Here
primeval symbolism from the history of religion is adopted
(although the Fathers did not talk about a "theology of religions", they put it into practice), in which the moon, being
a symbol of both fruitfulness and frailty, a symbol of death
and transience as well as a symbol of hope for rebirth and
resurrection, was an image of human existence, "pathetic
and comforting at the same time".[4] Lunar and terrestrial
symbolism fuse in many respects. The moon, in both its
transience and its rebirth, represents the world of men, the
earthly world, the world that is characterized by receptivity
and neediness, that receives its fruitfulness from somewhere
else: from the sun. Thus lunar symbolism simultaneously is
a symbol for man, for humanity as represented in woman:
receptive and fruitful due to the power of what is received.

The application of the moon symbolism to the Church by
the Fathers proceeded mainly from two points of departure:
from the connection between moon and woman (mother)
and from the viewpoint that the light of the moon is bor-
rowed light, the light of *helios*, without which the moon
would be mere darkness; it shines, yet its light is not its
own light but, rather, the light of another.[5] It is darkness

[4] M. Eliade, *Die Religionen und das Heilige* (Salzburg, 1954), 215; see
in general the whole chapter in that book entitled "Mond und Mond-
mystik", 180–216.

[5] See H. Rahner, *Griechische Mythen in christlicher Deutung* (Darmstadt,
1957), 200–224; H. Rahner, *Symbole der Kirche* (Salzburg, 1964), 89–
173. He makes the interesting remark that in antiquity natural science
thoroughly discussed the question of whether the moon has its own light

and brightness at the same time. The moon itself is darkness, but it bestows brightness that comes from another heavenly body whose light it transmits. Precisely therein, however, it represents the Church, which shines, even though she herself is dark: she is not bright because of her own light, but, rather, she receives light from the true *Helios*, Christ, so that she, although herself only earthly stone (like the moon, which, after all, is just another earth), nevertheless can give light in the night of our exile from God: "The moon tells of the mystery of Christ."[6]

One should not force symbols; they are valuable precisely because of their figurative nature, which eludes logical schematization. Nevertheless, in the age of the lunar voyage, an extension of the comparison comes to mind, in which the specific features of our situation (with regard to the reality "Church", also) can be made visible through this juxtaposition of physical and symbolic thinking. The traveler to the moon or the moon probe discovers the moon only as rocks, desert, sand, mountains, but not as light. And, in fact, in and of itself, it is nothing more, only desert, sand, and rocks. And yet it is also light—not in itself, but from another source and to another purpose—and it remains so even in the age of space travel. It is what it itself is not. The other thing that is not its own is nevertheless its reality, also —as what is "not its own". There is a truth of physics, and there is a truth of poetry, of symbols, and neither cancels the other out. And now I ask: Is this not a very exact image of the Church? Someone who drives over her and extracts

---

or some other. Most of the Church Fathers subscribed to the latter theory, which had become the predominant one, and attributed symbolic theological value to it (see esp. p. 100).

[6] Ambrose, *Exameron* IV 8, 23 CSEL 32, 1, p. 137, ll. 27f.; H. Rahner, *Griechische Mythen*, 201.

samples with a moon probe can discover only desert, sand,
and rocks, the human frailties of man and his history with
its deserts, its dust, and its heights. That is hers. And yet
it is not the essential thing about her. The decisive thing is
that she, although only sand and stone herself, nevertheless
is light from the Lord, from someone else: what is not hers
is what is truly and properly hers; indeed, her nature lies in
the fact that she herself does not count, but, rather, what
counts about her is what she is not, that she exists only so
as to be dispossessed of herself—the fact that she has a light
that she is not and solely on account of which she nevertheless is. She is "moon"—*mysterium lunae*—and thus she
matters to the believer, because in precisely this way she is
the place of a lasting spiritual decision.

Because the state of affairs touched on in this image seems
to me to be crucial, I would like to clarify it by means of
another observation before I try to translate it from the language of imagery into objective statements. After the liturgy
was translated into German [*ad experimentum*, as part of the
liturgical movement] before the recent [postconciliar] reform, I repeatedly had linguistic scruples about one passage
that came from the same context and symptomatically illus-
trates once more just what we have been talking about. The
Suscipiat in German prays that the Lord might accept the sacrifice "zum Segen für uns und *Seine* ganze heilige Kirche"
(as a blessing for us and for all *His* holy Church). Again and
again I found myself saying, "and for all *our* holy Church".
The whole problem we are discussing lies revealed in this linguistic scruple, and it makes evident the whole shift we have
experienced. His Church has been replaced by our Church
and, thus, by many churches, since everyone has his own.
The churches have become *our* undertakings, of which we
are either proud or ashamed; many little private properties

stand in a row, genuine "our" churches, which we ourselves make, which are our work and property, and which we try to refashion or preserve accordingly. Behind "our church" or even "your church", "his Church" has disappeared from view. But that is the only one that matters, and if she no longer exists, "our" church should resign too. Church as ours and ours alone is a pointless game in a sandbox.

Joseph Ratzinger (then a professor) taking part in a study tour of Israel with opportunities to contact the local Christians, which was organized by the Catholic Academy in Bavaria; pictured here with Julius Cardinal Döpfner (left) on the Temple Mount in Jerusalem in February 1975 (Photograph: Academy Archive).

Why I Stay in the Church

But with that we have already given in principle the answer to the question about which I was asked to speak: I am in the Church because I believe that now as ever and irrevocably through us, "his Church" lives behind "our church" and that I can stand by him only if I stand by and stay in his Church. I am in the Church because, despite everything, I believe that she is at the deepest level not our but precisely "his" Church.

To put it quite concretely: It is the Church that, despite all the human foibles of the people in her, gives us Jesus Christ, and only through her can we receive him as a living, authoritative reality that summons and endows me here and now. Henri de Lubac formulated this state of affairs as follows:

> Even those who scarcely know her or misunderstand her, do they realize that if they still receive Christ it is to the Church they owe it? . . . Jesus lives for us. But without the visible continuity of the Church, the desert sands would have long since swallowed up, if not perhaps his name and memory, certainly the influence of his gospel and faith in his divinity. . . . "Without the Church, Christ evaporates or is fragmented or cancels himself out." And without Christ what would man be?[7]

This elementary acknowledgment has to be made at the start: Whatever infidelity there is or may be in the Church, however true it is that she constantly needs to be measured anew by Jesus Christ, still there is ultimately no opposi-

---

[7] H. de Lubac, *Geheimnis aus der wir leben* (Einsiedeln, 1967), 20f.; cf. 18ff.

tion between Christ and Church. It is through the Church that he remains alive despite the distance of history, that he speaks to us today, is with us today as master and Lord, as our brother who unites us all as brethren. And because the Church, and she alone, gives us Jesus Christ, causes him to be alive and present in the world, gives birth to him again in every age in the faith and prayer of the people, she gives mankind a light, a support, and a standard without which mankind would be unimaginable. Anyone who wants to find the presence of Jesus Christ in mankind cannot find it contrary to the Church but only in her.

With that we have already made the next point. I am in the Church for the same reasons that I am a Christian in the first place. For one cannot believe alone. One can believe only as a fellow believer. Faith is by its very nature a force for unification. Its primordial image is the story of Pentecost, the miracle of understanding among people who by their origins and history are foreign to one another. Faith is ecclesial, or it is not faith. Furthermore: Just as one cannot believe alone but only as a fellow believer, neither can one believe on the basis of one's own authority and ingenuity, but only when there is an authorization to believe that is not within my power and does not come from me but, rather, goes before me. A faith of one's own devising is an oxymoron. For a self-made faith would only vouch for and be able to say what I already am and know anyway; it could not go beyond the boundary of my ego. Hence a self-made Church, a faith community that creates itself, that exists by its own graces, is also an oxymoron. Although faith demands communion, it is the sort of communion that has authority and takes the lead, not the sort that is my own creation, the instrument of my own wishes.

The whole matter can also be formulated in terms of a

more historical aspect: Either this Jesus was more than a man, so that he had an inherent authority that was more than the product of his own arbitrary will, or he was not. In other words, either an authority proceeded from him that extends and lasts through the ages, or else he left no such authority behind. In the latter case, I have to rely on my own reconstructions, and then he is nothing more than any other great founding figure that one makes present by reflection. But if he is more than that, then he does not depend on my reconstructions; then the authority that he left behind is valid even today.

Let us return to the crucial point: being Christian is possible only in Church. Not close by. And let us not hesitate to ask once more, quite soberly, the melodramatic question: Where would the world be without Christ? Without a God who speaks and knows man and whom man can therefore know? Nowadays the attempt to construct such a world is carried on with such grim obstinacy that we know quite precisely what the answer is: an absurd experiment. An experiment without any standard. However much Christianity may have failed in practice during its history (and it has failed again and again appallingly), the standards of justice and love have nevertheless emanated from the good news preserved in the Church, even against her will, often in spite of her, and yet never without the quiet power of what has been deposited in her.

In other words: I remain in the Church because I view the faith—which can be practiced only in her and ultimately not against her—as a necessity for man, indeed for the world, which lives on that faith even when it does not share it. For if there is no more God—and a silent God is no God—then there is no longer any truth that is accessible to the world and to man. In a world without truth, however, one cannot keep on living; even if we suppose that we can do without truth, we still feed on the quiet hope that it has not yet really disappeared, just as the light of the sun could remain for a while after the sun came to an end, momentarily disguising the worldwide night that had started.

We could express the same thing again differently from another perspective: I remain in the Church because only the Church's faith saves man. That sounds very traditional, dogmatic, and unreal, but it is meant quite soberly and realistically. In our world of compulsions and frustrations, the longing for salvation has reawakened with hurricane force. The efforts of Freud and C. G. Jung are just attempts to give redemption to the unredeemed. Marcuse, Adorno, and Habermas continue in their own way, from different starting points, to seek and proclaim salvation. In the background stands Marx, and his question, too, is the question of salvation. The more liberated, enlightened, and powerful man becomes, the more the longing for salvation gnaws at him, the less free he finds himself. The common element in the efforts of Marx, Freud, and Marcuse is that they look for salvation by striving for a world that is delivered from suffering, sickness, and need. A world free of dominion, suffering, and injustice has become the great slogan of our generation; the stormy protests of the young are aimed at this promise, and the resentments of the old rage against the fact that it has not yet been fulfilled, that there still is dominion, injustice, and suffering. To fight against suffering and injustice in the world is indeed a thoroughly Christian impulse. But the notion that one can produce a world without suffering through social reform, through the abolition of government and the legal order, and the desire to achieve that here and now are symptoms of false doctrine, of a profound misunderstanding of human nature. Inequality of ownership and

power, to tell the truth, are not the only causes of suffering
in this world. And suffering is not just the burden that man
should throw off: someone who tries to do that must flee
into the illusory world of drugs so as to destroy himself in
earnest and arrive at reality through the conflict. Only by
suffering himself and by becoming free of the tyranny of
egotism through suffering does man find himself, his truth,
his joy, his happiness. We are deceived to think that it is possible to become a human being without conquering oneself,
without the patience of renunciation and the toil of overcoming oneself; we are fooled to think there is no need for
the hardness of persevering in what has been undertaken
for enduring patiently the tension between what man ought
to be and what he is in fact: this is the very essence of the
crisis of the hour. Take away a man's hardship and lead him
astray into the fool's paradise of his dreams, and he loses
what is distinctively his: himself. A human being in fact is
saved in no other way but through the cross, through acceptance of his own passion and that of the world, which in
God's Passion became the site of liberating meaning. Only
in that way, in this acceptance, does a man become free. All
offers that promise it at less expense will fail and prove to
be deceptive. The hope of Christianity, the prospect of faith
is ultimately based quite simply on the fact that it tells the
truth. The prospect of faith is the prospect of truth, which
can be obscured and trampled upon, but cannot perish.

We come to our final point. A man always sees only as
much as he loves. Certainly there is also the clear-sightedness
of denial and hatred. But they can see only what is suited to
them: the negative. They can thereby preserve love from a
blindness in which it overlooks its own limitations and risks.
But they cannot build up. Without a certain measure of love,
one finds nothing. Someone who does not get involved at

least for a while in the experiment of faith, in the experiment of becoming affirmatively involved with the Church, who does not take the risk of looking with the eyes of love, is only exasperating himself. The venture of love is the prerequisite for faith. If it is ventured, then one does not have to hide from the dark areas in the Church. But one discovers that they are not the only thing after all. One discovers that alongside the Church history of scandals there is another Church history that has proved to be fruitful throughout the centuries in great figures such as Augustine, Francis of Assisi, the Dominican priest Las Casas, who fought passionately for the Indians, Vincent de Paul, and John XXIII. He finds that the Church has brought forth in history a gleaming path that cannot be ignored. And the beauty that has sprung up in response to her message and is still manifest to us today in incomparable works of art becomes for him a witness to the truth: something that could express itself in that way cannot be mere darkness. The beauty of the great cathedrals, the beauty of the music that has developed within the context of the faith, the dignity of the Church's liturgy, and in general the reality of festive celebration, which one cannot make for oneself but can only receive,[8] the elaboration of the seasons in the liturgical year, in which then and now, time and eternity interpenetrate—all that is in my view no insignificant accident. Beauty is the radiance of truth, Thomas Aquinas once said, and one might add that the distortion of the beautiful is the self-irony of lost truth. The lasting impression that the Christian faith was able to make upon history testifies to it, to the truth that stands behind it.

There is another point that I do not want to omit, even

---

[8] On this subject, see especially J. Pieper, *Leisure, the Basis of Culture*, trans. Alexander Dru (South Bend, Ind.: St. Augustine's Press, 1998).

though it seems to lead us into the realm of subjectivity. Even today, if you keep your eyes open, you can still meet people who are a living witness to the liberating power of the Christian faith. And there is nothing wrong with being and remaining a Christian, too, on account of the people who modeled Christianity for us and through their lives made it worth believing and loving. After all, it is an illusion when a person tries to make himself into a sort of transcendental subject in whom only that which is not accidental has any validity. Certainly there is a duty then to reflect on such experiences, to test their reliability, to purify them and comply with them anew. But even then, in this necessary process of making them objective, is it not a respectable proof of Christianity that it has made men human by uniting them with God? Is not the most subjective element here at the same time something completely objective for which we do not have to apologize to anyone?

One more remark at the conclusion. When we speak, as we have done here, about the fact one cannot see anything without love, that one must therefore also learn to love the Church in order to recognize her, many people today become uneasy: Is love not the opposite of criticism? And in the final analysis, is it not the subterfuge of the ruling powers that are trying to divert criticism and maintain the status quo for their own benefit? Do we serve mankind by reassuring it and putting a good face on the present situation, or do we serve it by standing up for it constantly against entrenched injustice and oppressive social structures? Those are very far-reaching questions that cannot be examined here in detail. But one thing ought to be clear: real love is neither static nor uncritical. If there is any possibility at all of changing another person for the better, then it is only by loving him and by slowly helping him to change from what he is into what he can be. Should it be any different with the Church? Just look at recent history: in the liturgical and theological renewal during the first half of the twentieth century, a real reform developed that brought about positive change; that was possible only because there were watchful individuals who, with the gift of discernment, loved the Church "critically" and were willing to suffer for her. If nothing succeeds any more today, maybe it is because all of us are all too intent on merely proving ourselves right. Staying in a Church that we actually have to make first in order for her to be worth staying in is just not worthwhile; it is self-contradictory. Staying in the Church because she is worth having around; because she is worth loving and transforming ever anew through love so that she transcends herself and becomes more fully herself—that is the path that the responsibility of faith shows us even today.

The Regent of the Catholic Academy in Bavaria at the evening reception on the Feast of Corpus Christi; June 9, 1977 (Photograph: Academy Archive/ Gerd Pfeiffer).

On the Global Task
of the Christian Faith

The question about the Christian foundation of the European self-concept and the related question about the duties of Christians in shaping the future of Europe were at the center of an international conference on "Europe and Christians" sponsored by the Catholic Academy in Bavaria and held in Strasbourg on April 28–29, 1979. The event took place immediately before the first direct election to the European Parliament; besides the political scientist Dolf Sternberger, the ambassador from the State of Israel to the German Federal Republic, Ehud Avriel, and the historian Joseph Rovan, the speakers included also the then-Archbishop of Munich and Freising, Joseph Cardinal Ratzinger. In his foundational lecture, he elaborated on the topic, starting with an analysis of the intellectual situation, continuing with a definition of the specifically European heritage, and concluding with a series of theses pointing the way to practical coexistence in a future Europe that will do justice to the noble claims of its tradition.

EUROPE: A HERITAGE WITH OBLIGATIONS FOR CHRISTIANS

In the vicissitudinous history of the concept and reality of "Europe", it is significant that the idea of Europe has made a conspicuous entrance whenever danger threatened "the peoples who were to be united under this collective concept".[1] This is true not only in our time, when, after two world wars, considering the destruction in the European world, the question about the West and about the restoration of a united Europe has become urgent. Heinz Gollwitzer pointed out that the passage of the term "Europe" from learned language into popular speech, which occurred as early as the beginning of the modern era, should probably be viewed not only as a result of the widespread influence of humanistic thought, which owed much to antiquity, but also as a reaction to the threat from the Turks.[2] Europe comes to know its identity most clearly when it is forcibly confronted with something that represents its very opposite. One can most readily approach the essence of a thing by determining first what it is not. The problem with the contemporary debate about Europe and also with the political struggle for Europe consists largely of the fact that it remains unclear what people actually mean by "Europe"

Translated by Michael J. Miller.

[1] H. Gollwitzer, "Europa, Abendland", in *Historisches Wörterbuch der Philosophie*, ed. J. Ritter (Basel and Stuttgart, 1972), 2:826.

[2] Ibid.

or intend it to be. Is it more than a somewhat nebulous romantic dream? Is it more than a community of political and economic interests for former world powers that have been pushed to the sidelines? What is actually meant by Europe must lie somewhere between nebulous idealism and a merely pragmatic community of interests. Only when it is more than both of these can it represent over the long term a real and, at the same time, an ideal goal for political action that is informed by morality. Mere *Realpolitik* without a formative, moral idea does not hold up; yet mere idealism that has no concrete political content remains ineffective and empty. Thus an initial thesis that can serve as a basis for this lecture might be formulated as follows: Only when the term "Europe" represents a synthesis of political reality and moral ideality can it become a dynamic force for the future.

Accordingly, we must look for a concept of Europe that fulfills these requirements. Methodologically, the history of European thought and of European reality itself has just offered us a way, namely, by finding out first from the counterimages what Europe is not. Then, in a second section, I will attempt to formulate the positive components of the concept "Europe". The third section will briefly define the tasks faced by someone who wants Europe.

I. Counterimages to Europe

When we begin to ascertain the counterimages to what, based on history and on the ethos preserved within it, must be called "Europe", I see three in particular, each of which represents a different historical departure from the historical dynamic of the European thing. First, today there is a strong, worldwide psychological and political trend that would like to go back in history to a time before the European element. It wants to cleanse history, so to speak, of the incursion of the European thing, which is regarded as an alienation from one's own thing or in general as the original sin of history, as the reason for the life-threatening crisis in which mankind finds itself today. Second, there is a forward-looking trend that outruns and escapes European history, as it were, continuing its trajectory in such a way as to loosen its intrinsic hold on traditional elements. Third, there is a trend that combines these two movements and thereby aims at a complete fusion of realism and ideal driving forces and thus also becomes the most drastic alternative blueprint to Europe.

In the following remarks, I will attempt to outline briefly these three trends, which, I believe, can mark off the boundaries of the concept "Europe".

1. *Back before Europe*

From the end of antiquity until well into the early modern era, Islam proved to be the real counterpart to Europe. The contrast between Europe and Asia, between *Erebos* (evening) and *Oriens* (sunrise),[3] which can be found as early as the sixth century before Christ in the writings of Hecataeus of Miletus and which was not meant as a merely geographic distinction, continues in modified form in this confrontation. From its very origins, Islam is in certain respects a return to a monotheism that does not accept the Christian turn to a God who has become man, and it likewise shuts itself off from Greek rationality and the resulting culture, which by way of the idea of God's Incarnation had become a component of Christian monotheism. Of course, one may object

---

[3] H. Treidler, "Europe", in *Der kleine Pauly, Lexikon der Antike*, 2:448.

that again and again over the course of history there has been rapprochement between Islam and the intellectual world of Greece, but it has never lasted. Above all, this means that the separation of faith and law, of religion and tribal authority, was not completed in Islam and cannot be accomplished without disturbing Islam at the very core. Put differently: the faith is presented in the form of a more or less archaic system of civil and penal laws and corresponding practices in everyday life. Islam is defined, not in terms of nationality, but, rather, by a legal system that fixes its ethnic and cultural features and at the same time sets limits to rationality where the Christian synthesis sees that reason has its place.[4]

Since the eighteenth century, Islam obviously had lost much of its political and moral importance, and from the nineteenth century on it increasingly came under the rule of European legal systems that considered themselves universally applicable because, as enlightened law, they had detached themselves from their Christian foundations and now presented themselves as pure, rational law. But, for that very reason, these legal systems are necessarily perceived as godless and contrary to the faith wherever Islam is or becomes alive as a faith. Considering the unity of religion and of ethnicity, they appear to be an attack that is both ethnic and religious, to be an alienation not only from what is one's own but from what is real. The combination of these two affronts causes the vehemence of the reaction we can observe today.

There are certainly many reasons for the intensification of this trend, but they cannot be discussed here in detail. Most importantly, on the one hand, the Arab world has grown stronger politically and economically, and, on the other hand, European rational law is in a crisis, now that it

[4] See, for example, the presentation by Ringgren-Ström, *Die Religionen der Völker* (Stuttgart, 1959), 98-142.

has completely relinquished its religious foundations and de facto runs the risk of turning into a rule of anarchy. The moment Europe calls its own spiritual foundations into question or abolishes them, separates itself from its history and declares it a cesspool, the response of a non-European culture can only be a radical reaction and a return to the time before the encounter with Christian values.

Furthermore, I consider this reaction of the Islamic world to be only the most visible and politically most effective segment of a movement that, in many varied forms, is powerfully at work within the European consciousness itself. The work of Lévi-Strauss—to mention only one example —expresses for its part the longing in the European mind to put its Christian domestication behind it, precisely as domestication—as slavery, in contrast with which the *monde sauvage* can be seen as the better world.[5]

On another level, granted, yet structurally related in many respects, is the cruelest and most terrifying form of a return to a pre-Christian world: what Germany experienced in the first half of the twentieth century and exhibited to the rest of mankind. For in keeping with its basic tendency, National Socialism was a renunciation of Christianity as alienation from the "beautiful" Germanic "savagery" and the desire to go back to a time before the Judeo-Christian "alienation", when such savagery was celebrated as the true culture.[6]

2. *Escape into the future*

A second antithesis to the historical and moral entity called Europe developed—quite unlike what has been described

[5] This notion is critically examined in a book by my student B. Adoukonou, *Jalons pour une théologie Africaine* (Paris: Lethielleux, 1980).

[6] On this subject, see, for example, R. Baumgartner, *Weltanschauungskampf im Dritten Reich* (Mainz, 1977).

thus far—from the nature of the European mind itself and probably should be characterized today as the prevalent finding in the political thought of the so-called Western world in general. Typical for Europe is the separation of faith and law (a separation with a Christian basis) that includes the rationality of law and its relative autonomy with respect to the religious realm but also, generally speaking, the duality of Church and State. While the political realm is subject to religiously based ethical norms, it does not have a theocratic constitution.

This independence of reason has led in the modern era with increasing rapidity to its total emancipation and to an unlimited autonomy of reason. Reason thereby assumes the form of positive reason, as Auguste Comte understood it, which takes as its only standard what is experimentally verifiable. The radical consequence of this, however, is that the entire realm of values, the entire realm of what "is above us", drops out of the sphere of reason, that the sole binding standard for reason and thus for man, politically as well as individually, becomes what "is under him", namely, the mechanical forces of nature that can be manipulated experimentally. Granted, God is not rejected absolutely, but he belongs to the realm of what is purely private and subjective. In a highly problematic essay that nevertheless frames the issue suggestively, Friedrich Wilhelm Bracht tries to depict the real revolution of 1789 as the fact that God ceased to be the public *summum bonum* (highest good), that he was replaced first by the nation and then, from 1848 on, by the proletariat or else the world revolution. In his opinion, one would have to say about modern consumer society that its God is its belly.[7] In a society, however, in which God can

---

[7] F. W. Bracht, "Die Abkehr von Gott in der Politik", *Zeitbühne* 8 (1979): 4–14, 41–48. I consider neither the political nor the ecclesial

no longer be the common, public *summum bonum* but is relegated to the private sphere, God's status is changed for the individual as well. A society in which the movement we have just described has taken over completely I would call "post-European". In such a society, the things that constituted Europe as a spiritual reality have been abandoned. In this sense, today's Western societies appear to me to be largely post-European societies already, which of course live on the aftereffects of the European heritage and to that extent are still European. The plurality of values that is legitimate and European is noticeably exaggerated into a pluralism that increasingly excludes every moral mainstay of law and every public embodiment of the sacred, of reverence for God as a value that is communal, too. Even to question this is considered, in most circles, an offense against tolerance and against the society founded on reason alone. But a society in which this is radically the case cannot, I am convinced, remain a society of law for long. It will open the door to tyranny when it is sufficiently weary of anarchy. Rudolf Bultmann, in a very astute analysis of the problem of law, which he undertakes within the context of his commentary on the trial of Jesus, formulates the extremely thought-provoking statement: "An unchristian State is possible in principle, but not an atheistic State."[8] Western societies are going through this learning experience today. The Islamic reaction against Europe is very closely connected with it, as we have already indicated.

---

notions of Bracht acceptable, but the question about God's position in public consciousness deserves attention, even if one cannot agree with the author on anything else.

[8] R. Bultmann, *The Gospel of John: A Commentary* (Oxford, 1971), 660f.

3. *Marxism*

The two trends described above are combined in a remarkable manner in Marxism, the third and most impressive form of turning away from the historical scheme of Europe. Marxism, on the one hand, harks back to a situation prior to Christian faith; it is a return to the salvation that was begun in Christ, an entrance into the still open-ended structure of Israel's hope. But it does so, not by anchoring itself in Israel's great religious heritage, but merely by drawing upon its religious dynamic and the full force of a hope that transcends rationality; then, however, it applies as its instrument the totally emancipated reason of the modern era, which has been freed from metaphysical connections of any sort. It sees its *summum bonum* in the world revolution, that is, in the total renunciation of the world as it has been until now, whereby the world that is to be newly created, as the negation of a negation, must be totally positive. Inasmuch as it combines the two countermovements to what is European, Marxism qualifies as the most radical antithesis not only to what is Christian as such, but also to the historical scheme that has been shaped by Christianity. What has been until now is viewed simply as an anti-value, and for that very reason the revolution is considered the absolute value. What has been until now takes its place in the historical process, once it has been understood, but that in no way alters the fact that overcoming it is the only progressive action possible that will lead history onward to its goal. Accordingly, Marxism is the product of Europe but at the same time the most decisive rejection of Europe, in the sense of that inner identity which it has developed over the course of its history.

II. Positive Components of the Concept of Europe

In the second section I will attempt to outline positively what Europe is. I intend to do so by examining the history of the meaning of the word "Europe", in which the inner stratification of the complex structure of Europe becomes visible. It seems to me that we can discern four such strata.

1. *The Greek heritage*

Europe, as a word and as a geographical and intellectual-spiritual concept, is a construct of the Greeks. The term in itself is indicative. It probably goes back to a name for evening (*ereb*) that was common to several Semitic languages and thus refers to the fateful dialogue of the Semitic mind and the Western mind, which belongs to the essence of what is European.[9] Geographically, the space described as Europe gradually widened. At first it included only the region of Thessaly, Macedonia, and Attica. As early as Herodotus, however, it was part of the threefold division of the earth into Europe, Asia, and Libya, one of the three great geographical and cultural zones that are contiguous in the region of the Mediterranean Sea.[10]

Europe, accordingly, appears to be constituted at first by the spirit of Greece. If it were to forget its Greek heritage, it could no longer be Europe. While the myth of Europa points to the area of the chthonic [underworld] religions and of Minoan religious circles, the formation of Europe was based on overcoming the chthonic religion through the Apollonian form. Greece is a heritage with obligations,

[9] Treidler, "Europe", 2:448.
[10] Ibid.

although they are difficult to describe in detail. I would regard as the central feature what Helmut Kuhn has called the Socratic difference: the difference between the good and goods and, thus, the difference in which both the right of conscience and also the reciprocal relation of *ratio* and *religio* are present.[11]

The heritage of Greece can also be formulated from another perspective that is somewhat more comprehensible to us. One of its discoveries, which is valid for all ages (despite the many different connotations of the term today), is democracy, which of course, as Plato explained, is essentially connected with *eunomia*, with the validity of good law, and which can remain democracy only in that connection.[12] Thus democracy is never merely majority rule, and the mechanism by which majorities are established must be subject to the common rule of the *nomos*, of what is intrinsically right, that is, to the recognition of values that are an obligatory prerequisite for the majority also.

2. *The Christian heritage*

The second stratum of the concept "Europe" becomes evident in the well-known episode in Acts 16:6–10. After this extremely odd and dramatic account, the Spirit of Jesus forbids Saint Paul to continue his missionary journey within the confines of Asia. Instead, a Macedonian appears to him in a vision one night and calls to him: "Come over to Macedonia and help us." The passage then continues: "And when he

[11] H. Kuhn, *Der Staat* (Munich, 1967), 25f.

[12] Cf. C. Meier, "Demokratie", in *Geschichtliche Grundbegriffe: Historisches Lexikon zur politisch-sozialen Sprache in Deutschland* (Stuttgart, 1973), 829ff.

had seen the vision, immediately we sought to go on into Macedonia, concluding that God had called us to preach the gospel to them." Although it is depicted in this way only in the Acts of the Apostles, I still think that this has a broader basis in the New Testament. In my opinion, what is being said here intrinsically touches upon a saying from the Gospel of John that occupies a significant place there. Before the Passion, after Jesus' entrance into Jerusalem, at the very moment when there is talk about the fulfillment of Jesus' glory, the request of the Greeks arrives: "Sir, we wish to see Jesus" (Jn 12:21). Bishop Graber has pointed out that in Saint Luke's account of Pentecost, in the list of peoples who represent the whole world (Acts 2:9ff.), only Asian peoples are named at first. Not until the very last place is there any mention of the Romans who are present.[13] The point of departure for the Gospel, therefore, is in the Orient. Like John and the whole New Testament, Luke emphasizes the root, which is Israel: salvation comes from the Jews (Jn 4:22). But Luke adds a path that opens up a new door. The path traced out in the Acts of the Apostles, all told, is a path from Jerusalem to Rome, a pathway to the pagans by whom Jerusalem is destroyed and who nevertheless adopt it in a new way.

Christianity, accordingly, is the synthesis brought about in Jesus Christ between Israel's faith and the Greek mind. Wilhelm Kamlah has portrayed this very impressively.[14] Europe is based on this synthesis. The Renaissance attempt to distill and restore the Greek element in a pure form by removing the Christian element is just as hopeless and absurd

---

[13] R. Graber, *Ein Bischof spricht über Europa* (Regensburg, 1978), 10f. and 22f., along with the reference to the relation to John 12:21.

[14] W. Kamlah, *Christentum und Geschichtlichkeit* (Stuttgart, 1951).

as the more recent attempt to manufacture a de-Hellenized Christianity. In my opinion, Europe in the narrower sense originates from this synthesis and is founded upon it.

3. *The Latin heritage*

A third stratum of the concept is evident in the fact that during the sixth century "Europe" was understood as a term for Gaul and that the Carolingian Empire then claimed to be Europe and to exhaust the meaning of this word.[15] In the further course of the development, this identification, which was never universally accepted, loosened up again to a great extent. An equation of the medieval *Imperium sacrum* with Europe did not result. The concept "Europe" was more capacious than that of the Holy Roman Empire, which considered itself to be the Christian transformation of the *Imperium Romanum*. On the contrary, Europe now coincided with the Occident, that is, with the sphere of the Latin culture and Church, whereby this Latin territory included not only the Romance peoples but also the Germanic, Anglo-Saxon, and some of the Slavic peoples, especially the Poles. The *res publica christiana*, which the Christian West considered itself to be, was not a politically constituted structure but, rather, a real and living whole in its cultural unity, in its "legal systems, which transcended tribes and nations, in its councils, in the institution of its universities, in the founding and spread of its religious orders, and in the circulation of its intellectual and ecclesial life through Rome as the ventricle of its heart".[16]

The medieval *res publica christiana* cannot be restored, and to restore it as such is not a reasonable goal, either. History

---

[15] Gollwitzer, "Europa, Abendland", 826.
[16] Ibid., 825.

cannot be turned back. A future Europe must carry within itself the fourth dimension also, that of the modern era, and above all must surpass the all-too-narrow framework of the West, of the Latin world, so as to include the Greek world and the Eastern Christian world, or at least it will have to be open to them. But conversely, there can be no future Europe that would jettison the Latin heritage, the heritage of the Christian West in the sense that we have just described. If that were to happen, we would no longer be talking about Europe but would already have bid farewell to it.

4. *The heritage of the modern era*

As the fourth stratum of what constitutes Europe we should mention the indispensable contribution made by the spirit of the modern era. Granted, the ambivalence inherent in each of the individual strata is perhaps most plainly in evidence here. But by no means should this lead to a rejection of the modern era, a temptation that one could encounter both in nineteenth century Romanticism with its nostalgia for the Middle Ages and also in Catholic circles between the two world wars.

I consider it to be the characteristic feature of the modern era, in the positive sense, that the separation of faith and law, which in the medieval *res publica christiana* was rather hidden, is now carried out consistently; as a consequence, freedom of religion gradually and clearly takes shape in a variety of bourgeois legal systems, and, thus, the interior claims of the faith are distinguished from the fundamental claims of the ethos upon which the law is based. The human values that are fundamental for the Christian world view make it possible, in a productive dualism of Church and State, to have a free, humane society in which freedom of conscience and, with it, fundamental human rights are secured. In this society, different expressions of the Christian faith can coexist and make room for different political positions, which nevertheless have in common a central set of standard values, the binding force of which simultaneously safeguards a maximum of freedom.

As we know from our own experience, this is a rather idealized picture of the modern era, as it wanted to see itself but never quite was concretely. The ambivalence of the modern era is based on the fact that it obviously failed to appreciate the roots and the real-life basis of the idea of freedom and urged an emancipation of reason that intrinsically contradicts the nature of human reason (which is not divine) and therefore necessarily became unreasonable itself. The epitome of the modern era appears—wrongly, in the final analysis—to be that completely autonomous reason which no longer recognizes anything but itself and has thereby gone blind and, through the destruction of its own foundations, becomes inhumane and hostile to creation. This sort of autonomous reason is, granted, the product of the European mind, but at the same time it should be regarded as essentially post-European, indeed anti-European, as the inner destruction of what is not only constitutive for Europe but is the prerequisite for humane society in general. Thus, we must adopt from the modern era, as an essential and indispensable dimension of what is European, the relative separation of Church and State, freedom of conscience, human rights, and reason's responsibility for itself, while resisting its radicalization by holding fast to the foundations of reason in reverence for God and for the fundamental moral values that come from the Christian faith.

III. Theses for a Future Europe

From the discussion thus far it is probably clear that not every political or economic union that takes place in Europe constitutes per se Europe's future. A mere centralization of business or legislative jurisdictions can also lead to an accelerated deconstruction of Europe, if it leads, for instance, to a technocracy that takes increased consumption as its sole standard. Conversely, such institutions have their value in a larger context as a way of overcoming nation-worship and as part of a peaceful order in which all have a share in this world's goods. Of course, then, their fundamental rule cannot be an extended group-egotism of the rich nations as they defend their advantages. Their shared wealth must be understood as a shared responsibility for the world as a whole, and in this sense Europe has to be an open-ended system in its economic mechanisms as well. The idea of ruling the world and of dividing up the other parts of the world into colonies must be replaced by the idea of an open society and of reciprocal responsibility. This fundamental orientation, which results from the concept of Europe that has been elaborated thus far, can be developed in four theses from the four dimensions of Europe I have tried to outline.

First thesis: One constitutive element of Europe from its beginnings in Hellas is the intrinsic correlation of democracy and *eunomia*, that is, laws that cannot be manipulated.

As opposed to party rule and dictatorship (arbitrary rule), Europe has had a high regard for the rule of reason and of freedom, which can last only as the rule of law. The limitation of power, checks on power, and transparency in wielding power are constitutive elements of the European community. As a prerequisite for these, the law must be immune to manipulation and must have its own inviolable sphere of action. The prerequisite for this, in turn, is what the Greeks called *eunomia*, which means that the law is based on moral standards. Therefore, I consider it undemocratic to turn the expression "law and order" into abusive language. Every dictatorship begins with disparagement of the law. We should agree with Plato also when he says that it is less important to have a particular type of mechanism for forming the majority than it is to actualize as securely as possible under the given circumstances the *content* of democratic mechanisms, that is, the control of power by law, the inviolability of law by those in power, and the normalization of law in accordance with ethics. Accordingly, anyone who fights for Europe is fighting for democracy, but for democracy in its indissoluble connection with *eunomia*, as the concept has just been described.

Second thesis: If *eunomia* is the prerequisite for the viability of democracy, as opposed to tyranny and mob rule, then the fundamental prerequisite for *eunomia* in turn is a common—and, for public law, obligatory—reverence for moral values and for God.

Once more I recall Bultmann's important statement: "An unchristian State is possible in principle, but not an atheistic State"—at least, not as a State that simultaneously continues to be ruled by law. This implies that God is *by no means* relegated to the private sphere but is recognized publicly also as the supreme value. This certainly includes—and I would like to emphasize this very strongly—tolerance and a place for the atheist, and it must have nothing to do with coercion in matters of faith. It is just that, the way things are beginning to develop now, in many respects they should be the other way around: atheism is starting to be the fundamental public dogma, and faith is tolerated as a private opinion, yet this arrangement ultimately does *not* tolerate faith in its essence. Ancient Rome, too, granted such private tolerance to faith; sacrificing to Caesar was supposed to be only an admission that faith had no public rights and, in any case, made no fundamental claim.

I am convinced that in the long term the rule of law has no chance of survival in a State that is radically and dogmatically atheistic and that it is necessary to reconsider this question fundamentally—as a matter of survival. I likewise venture to declare that democracy is capable of functioning only when conscience is functioning and that the latter has nothing to say if it is not oriented to the validity of the fundamental moral values of Christianity, which can be put into action even without a Christian profession of faith, indeed, even in the context of a non-Christian religion.

Third thesis: The rejection of the dogma of atheism as a prerequisite for public law and the formation of a State, along with a publicly recognized reverence for God as the basis for ethics and law, means rejecting both the nation and also the world revolution as the *summum bonum*.

Nationalism not only brought Europe to the brink of destruction de facto and historically; it also contradicts what Europe essentially is, spiritually and politically—even though it has dominated recent decades of European history. Hence international political, economic, and legal institutions are necessary; these naturally cannot be intended as building blocks for a super-nation but instead should restore and strengthen the proper identity and importance of the individual regions of Europe. Regional, national, and supranational institutions should mesh in such a way that both centralism and particularism are excluded in like manner. Above all, open exchange and unity in variety should be revitalized to a great extent through nongovernmental cultural and religious institutions and forces.

In the universities, religious orders, and Church councils, the Middle Ages were acquainted with European institutions as a concrete, nongovernmental reality that was effective precisely as such. Recall that Anselm of Canterbury, for instance, came from Aosta in Italy and served as abbot in Brittany and as archbishop in England; that Albert the Great came from Germany and was able to teach just as well in Paris as in Cologne and then became the bishop of Regensburg; that Thomas Aquinas taught in Naples, Paris, and Cologne and that Duns Scotus was an instructor in England as well as in Paris and Cologne, to mention only a few examples. There should be a revival of this; if these cultural entities are not decisively strengthened as vital, nongovernmental institutions, then in my opinion the merely governmental and economic mechanisms can ultimately have no positive effect. From this perspective, Christian ecumenism has a specifically European significance, too. Just as nationalism is opposed to the future of Europe, so too does Marxism, at least in its pure form, contradict what is essential to Europe. Its rejection of history, which in its entirety is demoted to the status of a mere prehistory of the world that is yet to be created, its methods, and its goals lead to a tyrannical society in which law and ethics can be manipulated and, therefore, freedom is turned into its opposite.

Fourth thesis: For Europe, the recognition and the preservation of freedom of conscience, human rights, academic freedom, and hence of a free human society must be constitutive.

These achievements of the modern era should be safeguarded and developed, without falling into the bottomless pit of a rationalism devoid of transcendence, which abolishes its own freedom from within. By these standards the Christian will evaluate European policy, and based on them he will fulfill his political task.

On June 27, 1982, at its annual celebration in Munich, the Catholic Academy in Bavaria observed the twenty-fifth anniversary of its founding by the seven Bavarian dioceses. The centerpiece of the event was the lecture reprinted here, which was given by Joseph Cardinal Ratzinger, who at that time had been Prefect of the Congregation for the Doctrine of the Faith for around seven months. His reflections on the task of a Catholic academy extended far beyond the immediate occasion and defined the relation between dialogue, freedom, and truth for our understanding of academic life. At the same time, in view of the presentation of the Romano Guardini Prize to the Carmelite nun Sister Gemma Hinricher, O.C.D., the talk described the much wider arc leading to the question of the relation between academic endeavor and contemplation and the outstanding significance of Christian contemplation as an essential way of interpreting the world.

INTERPRETATION—
CONTEMPLATION—ACTION

Reflections on the Mission of a Catholic Academy

In awarding the Romano Guardini Prize year after year, the Catholic Academy in Bavaria reflects on its own foundations and mission. The great figure of Romano Guardini, the Christian interpreter of the world and the times, appears before it again as its standard and guide. The slogan "interpretation of the world" calls to mind its substantial mission, which the 1956 prospectus summed up in the following words: "The task of the Catholic Academy can be comprehensively defined as an encounter of the Catholic faith with today's world in its various outward manifestations of theoretical knowledge and practical life-style."[1] Meanwhile, the distinguished series of Guardini Prize recipients has itself become a commentary on the expression "interpretation of the world" and, thus, of the academy's intention; the prize-winners have become an eloquent indication of how multiform the approaches to this interpretation can and must be, given the dimensions of world and man that are involved. Philosophical and theological reflection, artistic creation, contemplation—these can all be ways and means of interpreting the world.

Translated by Adrian Walker and Michael J. Miller.

[1] B. Zittel, *Gründungsgeschichte der Katholischen Akademie in Bayern* (Munich, 1982), document 25, p. 118.

At the same time, this also suggests the inexhaustible character of the topic assigned to me this evening; obviously, there is no way to treat it adequately in a lecture when even such multiform careers and accomplishments, for their part, can manage to do so only in segments, each in its own way, with its limitations and its richness. That means that I am free to make a selection, which ultimately can only be fortuitous. So I will let what is special about this occasion determine the path that I take: the remembrance inherent in this hour as well as the present and particular features that distinguish it. The remembrance concerns the formation of the Academy twenty-five years ago and its history since then, along with the questions that have accompanied it and the influence that it has been privileged to have. Since the task assigned to me tonight is not to chronicle events but, rather, to search for the reason that gave rise to it and opens up its future, the questions are more important than reflection on what has happened. From the beginning there were two objections, of varying intensity at different times, against the idea and the reality of a Catholic Academy; these objections are in many respects contrary, yet in many ways closely related also. On the one hand, people might ask: Are academies of this sort really in keeping with the Church's mission? Do they not lead all too easily to a flight from the faith into ingenious talks about the faith, into that "dulling of the spirit by wittiness" about which Goethe spoke?[2] Would not the really appropriate thing be a place for actualization: a retreat house, for instance, where one does not think *about*

---

[2] *Maximen und Reflexionen*, Kröner's paperback edition, ed. G. Müller, no. 944; cited here from J. Pieper, *Was heißt akademisch?* 2nd ed. (Munich, 1964), 47. Now as before, I think that this little book, which was first published in 1952, is of fundamental importance for the question about things "academic"; my lecture is indebted to it for crucial guidance.

the faith but rather the faith itself is meditated, exercised, and put into practice? Here, then, the academic proves to be in contrast to the contemplative. An ancient explanation and danger of the academic comes into view, which goes back to the time of the so-called middle academy and, thus, to the pre-Christian era and is echoed in the title of Augustine's book *Against the Academics*. For him, getting free of what is merely academic was one stage along the way to becoming specifically Christian. This poses the question of the relation between the academic and the contemplative, the place of contemplation in the academy and its interpretation of the world. History passes into the present: the questions of the beginning touch on this evening's special occasion, on which an award will be given to the representative of a contemplative order, and thus contemplation, too, as a matter of principle should be mentioned as an essential way of interpreting the world.

Perhaps many of those who viewed academies as superfluous places for theory were less concerned about contemplation than about a certain pastoral pragmatism that wanted to see concrete action and results rather than reflection. Indeed, my whole talk this evening is aimed at demonstrating that the pragmatic objection to the academy is overcome when we recognize that contemplation is the core of spiritual actualization and at the same time understand that what is truly academic leads to the contemplative and cannot continue to exist without it. But that is getting ahead of ourselves; first, I should say that in pragmatism the seeming objection of piety encounters the critique of the impious, which in turn can be orchestrated in extremely different ways. For example, the question is asked: What does the freedom of such an academy mean? Is it not an empty and therefore rather dangerous alibi of ecclesiastical authority (read: the hierarchy), which can now say, "See, now, we do want and approve of a forum for free discussion", whereas in reality it is just a well fenced in, risk-free playing field that makes a nice impression but is inconsequential? Here, too, what is really at work is not concern about freedom but rather a question about the potential of such an enterprise to bring about change. This means that the inquiry is not academic, in the classical sense, but rather thoroughly pragmatic—in which the notions of the change for which we are striving can be widely divergent. This criticism of a sort of activity that is essentially aimed at interpretation touches on the question that since Marx has been omnipresent: whether we are not doing too little in the first place by interpreting and should instead be bringing about change. Certainly Karl Marx was the first to formulate this question so keenly and programmatically, but as a matter of fact it goes back to the basis of modern thought, when Francis Bacon in his *Novum Organum*, the new logic of the future, disavows the question of truth as the old, outmoded question and transforms it into the question of know-how, the question about power. The aim of philosophy is now no longer to understand being but, rather, to make ourselves "maîtres et possesseurs de la nature" (masters and owners of nature).[3] Whereas earlier the term "contemplation" emerged as the antithesis of "interpretation", at this juncture "action" now sets itself up in opposition to it. My reflections this evening will revolve around these three terms. In other words, we will ask how

[3] Cf. Pieper, *Was heißt akademisch?* 20. The significance of Bacon in the intellectual upheaval of the modern age is explained strikingly by M. Kriele, *Befreiung und politische Aufklärung* (Herder, 1980), 78–82; see also R. Spaemann and R. Löw, *Die Frage Wozu?* (Munich and Zürich, 1981), 13; 100f.

the academy, as a place of interpretation, should be understood in the contrasting light of contemplation and action.

So we should ask about the academy and academic pursuits: What are they really? When we look at the history of the word and the reality "academy" from Plato to the present, we see that there can be no answer based on the statistics of the lowest common denominator, so to speak; the only meaningful question is the one that inquires into the foundational force that again and again lent significance to academic pursuits, as culture changed and regimes came and went, and made it into that distinguished force of Western culture that can and must have permanent value in a global culture as well. It seems to me, though, that the answer, which ultimately is very simple, can be discovered only by a careful approach to what is essential, the unfathomable depths of which might otherwise remain hidden behind hackneyed expressions.

I. Of What Does an Academy Consist?

1. *Dialogue*

Let us begin with a fact that, though situated close to the surface of the matter, is more than an external detail. The academy, as Plato conceived it, is first and foremost a place of dialogue. But what does the word "dialogue" really mean? After all, *dialogue* does not take place simply because people are talking. Mere talk is the deterioration of dialogue that occurs when there has been a failure to reach it. Dialogue first comes into being where there is not only speech but also listening. Moreover, such listening must be the medium of an encounter; this encounter is the condition of an inner contact that leads to mutual comprehension. Reciprocal understanding, finally, deepens and transforms the being of the interlocutors. Having enumerated the single elements of this transaction, let us now attempt to grasp the significance of each in turn.

The first element is listening. What takes place here is an event of opening, of becoming open to the reality of other things and people. We need to realize what an art it is to be able to listen attentively. Listening is not a skill, like working a machine, but a capacity simply to be that puts in requisition the whole person.

To listen means to know and to acknowledge another and to allow him to step into the realm of one's own "I". It is readiness to assimilate his word, and therein his being, into one's own reality as well as to assimilate oneself to him in corresponding fashion. Thus, after the act of listening, I am another man, my own being is enriched and deepened because it is united with the being of the other and, through it, with the being of the world.

All of this presupposes that what my dialogue partner has to say does not concern merely some object falling within the range of empirical knowledge and of technical skills, that is, of external know-how. When we speak of dialogue in the proper sense, what we mean is an utterance wherein something of being itself, indeed, the person himself, becomes speech. This does not merely add to the mass of items of knowledge acquired and of performances registered but touches the very being of man as such, purifying and intensifying his potency to be who he is.

But a further dimension of dialogue, which pertains both to listening and to speaking, thus discloses itself. This is an element upon which the early Augustine set particular value. In fact, we can easily trace the story of Augustine's conversion in the records of his dialogues with his friends, in which the little academy of Cassiciacum groped its way toward the hour when a new word, which had been unknown to Plato, could at last tumble into its midst and become the beginning of a new life. Analyzing these colloquies in retrospect, Augustine concludes that the community of friends was capable of mutual listening and understanding because all of them together heeded the interior master, the truth.[4] Men are capable of reciprocal comprehension because, far from being wholly separate islands of being, they communicate in the same truth. The greater their inner contact with the one reality that unites them, namely, the truth, the greater their capacity to meet on common ground. Dialogue without this interior obedient listening to the truth would be nothing more than a discussion among the deaf.

Here we come upon a circumstance that, aside from its extraordinary importance in today's debate, at the same time reveals the perils to which dialogue is exposed. The capacity to reach a consensus presupposes the existence of a truth common to all. Consensus, however, must not try to pass itself off as a substitute for the truth. Let us stop at this point, which has led us right to the heart of the matter, in order to reflect upon a second characteristic of the "academic".

2. *Freedom*

From the very beginning, freedom has belonged to the essence of the academy and of its search for understanding. In this context, freedom means essentially two things. In the first place, it is the possibility to think everything, ask

---

[4] On the philosophy of the early Augustine, see, for example, E. König, *Augustinus philosophus: Christlicher Glaube und philosophisches Denken in den Frühschriften Augustins* (Munich, 1970).

everything, and say everything that appears worthy of being thought, asked, and said in the effort to find the truth.[5] So far, we are quite obviously within the range of what everyone today accepts and defends, at least in theory. Nonetheless, the question imposes itself: What justifies this freedom, which under certain circumstances can be so dangerous? What is its basis? What do we take this risk for? The answer, at least the only satisfying one, is that the truth itself, the truth for its own sake, is so precious that it warrants such a risk; otherwise, no one could dare to undertake it. However, we thereby immediately find ourselves in a dramatic conflict with all strategies of change and, at the same time, at the heart of the question concerning the foundation of our society in general. Let us attempt, therefore, to describe this point as precisely as possible. Josef Pieper defines it in the following manner: "The distinctive feature [of the academic] is above all this freedom from the necessity of pursuing some profit aim—this is authentic 'academic freedom', which, accordingly, is *per definitionem* wiped out as soon as the academic disciplines become mere technicians pursuing the objectives of some power interest of whatever sort."[6] "You can certainly believe that you have taken philosophy into your service; but behold, what has been taken into service is not philosophy."[7]

The question of freedom is inseparably linked to the question of truth. When truth is not a value in itself that merits both active interest and the expenditure of time indepen-

---

[5] In relation to this section, see J. Ratzinger, "Freedom and Constraint in the Church", in Ratzinger, *Church, Ecumenism, and Politics: New Endeavors in Ecclesiology*, trans. Michael J. Miller et al. (San Francisco, 2008), 175–92.

[6] Pieper, *Was heißt akademisch?* 28.

[7] Ibid., 29.

dently of its results, profit can be the only criterion with which to evaluate knowledge. If this is the case, knowledge has its *raison d'être* no longer in itself but in the objectives that it serves. It then belongs to the domain of ends and means. In other words, in one form or another it is subordinate to power and its acquisition. We can put it in yet another way: if man were absolutely incapable of knowing the truth itself but only the fitness for use that things have in view of particular aims, use and consumption would become the measure of all action and thought. In consequence, the world would no longer be anything but "material for praxis". We are thus in a position to see clearly the inexorable and ineluctable fundamental alternative, which to an ever greater extent has become *the* dilemma of the modern age, so that today it poses itself as the question upon which the whole destiny of our epoch hinges: Is truth accessible to man at all? Is the search for it worthwhile? Can we even say that the quest for truth and the knowledge that the truth is the lawful mistress of man are perhaps our only hope of salvation? Or is the final adieu to the whole business of truth, which emerges clearly in Francis Bacon's new logic, man's true liberation, which awakens him from his speculative reverie and allows him at last to take in his own hands the dominion over reality, in order to become "master and lord of nature"? Which is right: Giambattista Vico's definition, according to which truth is exclusively what has been produced (and therefore what can be produced), or the Christian option that truth is prior to making?[8] The freedom that derives from Bacon's new thinking is the freedom to produce everything and to acknowledge no other lawfulness save man's capacity to do. Such freedom had certainly not been recognized previously

---

[8] See J. Ratzinger, *Introduction to Christianity*, trans. J. R. Foster, 2nd ed. (San Francisco, 2000), 57–69.

and could set itself up as the true liberation, like the younger son, who takes possession of his own inheritance and sets out with it into the unknown. But the freedom to produce everything, which no longer perceives any obligation in the truth—the father—is subject to the constraint that from now on using and being used alone hold sway over man. When all is said and done, therefore, it is a slave's freedom —even though it reveals its true nature only late in the game and even though it takes a long time before it has so ruined itself by bad management that it lands among the pigs' husks and must still envy the swine because they are not cursed with freedom. The most advanced outposts of modern spiritual evolution have already reached this point. On the other hand, the ecological outcry against man as the destroyer of nature is no solution as long as it does not include a renewal of the quest for the truth. "The truth shall make you free" (Jn 8:32)—today we are ready for a completely fresh appreciation of the immeasurable claim and the power of this saying of the Lord. The real choice of our time has become that between the freedom of production and the freedom of the truth. But the freedom to produce, unchecked by truth, means the dictatorship of ends in a world devoid of truth and thus enslaves man while appearing to set him free. Only when truth has value in itself and a glimpse of it outweighs every success, only then are we free; and this is why the only authentic freedom is the freedom of the truth.

3. *The center: Truth as the basis and measure of freedom*

This brings us to the truly decisive point of our reflections: "academic" freedom is freedom for the *truth*, and its justification is simply to exist for the sake of the truth, without having to look back toward the objectives it has reached.

As she directs her gaze backward, Lot's wife is turned into a pillar of salt; Orpheus, climbing up to the light, lost everything when he glanced backward to assure himself of his success.[9] We will have to return to these connections when we turn to the theme of contemplation. The point of contact between the academic and the contemplative, the Platonic and the Christian becomes quite conspicuous here.

But first let us make the attempt to express the idea itself as precisely as possible, in order to see as clearly as we can both the claim and the consequences it entails. It seems to me a significant fact that Romano Guardini, with his characteristic perspicacity and uncompromising honesty, formulated this idea in connection with the Jewish question. This is no accident, for then, in the darkest days of the Third Reich, the deadliness of the alliance of reason, the machine, and politics had become fully manifest. What reason becomes when practical aims and the power of technique have been made the only god was by then plain for all to see; so too was the fact that only the continued authority of the truth, only its inviolability, offered hope of salvation. What Guardini said at that time concerning the university remains a valid manifesto of the authentically academic spirit: "If the university has a spiritual significance, it is to be the place of inquiry after the truth, for truth alone—not for an ulterior end, but for its own sake: simply because it is truth."[10] Bishop Hermann Dietzfelbinger, on the occasion of his acceptance of the Romano Guardini Prize, expressed the same thought in relation to present-day concerns. In the course of his speech, he pointed out that a shift has taken place from

[9] This image is to be found in Pieper, *Was heißt akademisch?* 69, who borrows it from K. Weiss.

[10] Guardini, *Verantwortung: Gedanken zur jüdischen Frage* (Munich, 1952), 10.

the question of truth to the question of value and went on to recall that the ideas of nascent National Socialism had managed to legitimate themselves under the guise of constructive and liberating "values". The statement of Carl Friedrich von Weizsäcker that the bishop cited in his speech deserves to be repeated here: "I maintain that in the long run only a truth-oriented society, not a happiness-oriented society, can succeed."[11]

However, if we bear in mind the context of the abovementioned saying of Guardini, this means that the most effective defense of man, as well as the best defense and purification of the world, is accomplished by resisting the hegemony of the dogma of change, indeed, the dogma of producibility in general, and by holding fast to the rights of truth for its own sake. For in becoming true, man contributes to the world's becoming true. Moreover, if man becomes true, he also becomes good, and the world likewise becomes good around him. Thomas Aquinas, as is well known, defined truth as the adequation of the intellect to reality. The personalistic philosophy of the inter- and postwar periods has been foremost in stressing quite sharply the inadequacy of this definition.[12] Though it is certainly the case that this formula does not say everything that can be said, it does bring to light something of decisive importance: the perception of the truth is a process that brings man into conformity with being. It is a becoming one of the "I" and the world, it is consonance, it is being gifted and purified. To the extent that men allow themselves to be guided and cleansed by the

[11] H. Dietzfelbinger, "Dimensionen der Wahrheit", in *Katholische Akademie in Bayern, Chronik, 1980/81*, 148–56; citation on 150.

[12] See L. B. Puntel, "Wahrheit", in H. Krings, H. M. Baumgartner, and C. Wild, *Handbuch philosophischer Grundbegriffe* 3 (Munich, 1974), 1649–68.

truth, they find the way not only to their true selves but also to the human "thou". Truth, in fact, is the medium in which men make contact, whereas it is the absence of truth that closes them off from one another. Accordingly, movement toward the truth implies temperance. If the truth purifies man from egotism and from the illusion of absolute autonomy, if it makes him obedient and gives him the courage to be humble, it thereby also teaches him to see through producibility as a parody of freedom and to unmask undisciplined chatter as a parody of dialogue. It is victorious over the tendency to mistake the absence of all ties for freedom. Thus, the truth is fruitful precisely by being loved for its own sake.

These considerations prepare us for a final step. We must still ask Pilate's question: What is truth? Nevertheless, we must ask it differently than Pilate did. Hermann Dietzfelbinger has pointed out that the depressing thing about Pilate's question is that it is not really a question at all but an answer. Pilate's response to the One who claims to have the truth is: "Enough talk—what is truth anyway? Let's deal with the concrete instead." For the most part, Pilate's question is posed in the same form today. We, however, must now formulate it in all seriousness: How is it that to become true is to become good and that truth is good, indeed, *the* good? How is it that the truth has value of itself, without having to validate itself with reference to exterior aims? These affirmations are correct only if the truth possesses its worth in itself, if it subsists in itself and has more being than everything else; if the truth itself is the ground upon which I stand. To think through the essence of truth is to arrive at the notion of God. In the long run, it is impossible to maintain the unique identity of the truth, in other words, its dignity (which in turn is the basis of the dignity both of man and of the world), without learning to perceive in it the unique identity and dignity of the living God. Ultimately, therefore, reverence for the truth is inseparable from that disposition of veneration which we call adoration. Truth and worship stand in an indissociable relationship to each other; one cannot really flourish without the other, however often they have gone their separate ways in the course of history.

4. Cult

This brings us to a final perspective in our investigation of the academy and its theoretical justification. At first sight, the fact that the word "academy" was originally the name of a suburban temple precinct, which thus predates Plato's erection of his school there, may seem rather accidental to the history of the new institution. Closer examination reveals a deeper connection, which was not lost on the founder. For Plato's Academy was, from the legal point of view, a cultic association. Accordingly, the cultic veneration of the Muses was a stable component of its rhythm of life; there was an explicit ministry of preparing sacrifices.[13] This is much more than an adventitious circumstance, a concession, say, to the sociological structures of the times. The freedom for the truth and the freedom of the truth cannot exist without the acknowledgment and worship of the divine. Freedom from the obligation to yield a profit can be justified and can survive only if there is something truly withdrawn from man's utility and property, hence, if the higher property right and the inviolable prerogative of the divinity perdure. "The freedom of *theoria*", says Pieper in the spirit of Plato, "is defenseless and exposed—unless it appeals in a

[13] Pieper, *Was heißt akademisch?* 37f.; cf. H. Meinhardt, "Akademie", in J. Ritter, ed., *Historisches Wörterbuch der Philosophie* I (Basel/Stuttgart, 1971), 121–24.

special way to the protection of the gods."[14] Freedom from profit and emancipation from the aims of power find their deepest guarantee only in the absolute rights of the One who is not subordinate to any human power: in the freedom vis-à-vis the world that God both has and gives. For Plato, who was the first to express it philosophically, the freedom of the truth belongs not merely accidentally but essentially in the context of worship, of cult. Where the latter no longer exists, the former ceases as well. It goes without saying that worship is also nonexistent where cultic forms are indeed perpetuated but are reinterpreted as symbolic actions possessing a merely social significance. All of this means, however, that anarchic pseudo-freedom is at work behind every denial of the foundations of adoration, behind every refusal of the bond to the truth and of the demands it makes. These counterfeit freedoms, which predominate today, are the real menace to true freedom. To clarify the concept of freedom is one of the crucial tasks of the present day—if we care about the preservation of man and of the world.

II. What Goes into Christian Contemplation?

With this analysis of things academic and interpretive, as contrasted with what is action-oriented and pragmatic, we have already run into the middle of our third basic concept. Because of the special character of this evening, I will digress before the last set of reflections, which will finally address the theme of the contemplative, and once again interpolate a brief reference to the history of the academy. It is generally known that Plato's Academy was disbanded in A.D. 529 by Emperor Justinian because to the very end it adhered to the inseparable connection between the worship of the

[14] Ibid., 36.

gods and philosophy and thus had become a foreign body in the Christian world. Yet a good hundred years previously, Emperor Theodosius II had called a Christian academy into being that transposed the cultic content into a Christian key and thus considered itself Plato's better heiress. There is a direct path from this academy to the imperial university of Emperor Constantine Monomachus, which in turn was the prerequisite for the establishment of the first university in the West. I said that Emperor Theodosius founded the first Christian university, but that is not entirely accurate: the real foundress was a woman, his wife, Eudocia, who was the daughter of the leader of the Platonic Academy at the time, Plutarch of Athens, and thus rightly felt that she was carrying on the great heritage of Greek philosophy. Her poem about the magician Cyprian of Antioch is the source of the medieval Faust legend. So there is a confluence of many things here, even the contemplative aspect again, for the most profound influence on this woman was her encounter with the contemplative monasticism of her time.[15]

But let us return to our topic. Whereas in the Scholastic theology of the Middle Ages women played almost no role, their contribution to mystical theology is significant. Surely this is primarily due to the fact that Scholasticism and mysticism have different sociological contexts: in the one case the school, and in the other the monastery, which forms a community in divine and human things. Teresa of Avila, who is before our eyes in a special way this year and this evening, developed from these traditions; in a unique way she embodies the meaning of Christian contemplation, and perhaps only a woman could embody it so purely. Here of course we immediately find again a multitude of women on this path. From outside, some ask whether this mysticism was not in

[15] Cf. Pieper, *Was heißt akademisch?* 13f.; H. Homeyer, "Eudokia-Athenais", in *LThK* 3:1170.

many cases a pastime, a sort of substitute for involvement in shaping public affairs. From inside, there is the objection that contemplation misses what is authentically Christian. It leaves behind salvation history, the God who acts in history and calls us to action, as a stage for beginners; ultimately, it is no longer about Christ, who remains man for all eternity, and instead it is about going beyond history and humanity to a static view of the ahistorical eternal. Actually, only rank ignorance can speak this way, for the incarnational principle and the Paschal Mystery form the heart of Teresian piety at all levels.

There is no longer time to explain all of this; moreover, there is among us someone who is able to do so better than I can. I would just like to show in outline form that the foundational structural elements of things academic and interpretive, which we examined earlier, are at the same time the structural elements of Teresian contemplation. Thus we can see the dependence of the academic on the contemplative and the openness of the contemplative to what is truly academic, and the significance of both for the potential of humanity, for responding correctly to the challenges of the world; all of this can then be combined as an explanation of the program of the academy that we mentioned at the outset, as an interpretation of its path yesterday and today.[16]

1. *The dialogical character*

For Teresa, the linguistic form of dialogue has become an ontological and existential form, because her life in its fundamental movement has become prayer, a dialogue with him

[16] The following description of Teresian mysticism is based largely on the illuminating essay by U. M. Schiffers, "Der Unsinn einer Flucht vor Gott: Ermutigung des Sünders zum inneren Gebet", *Christliche Innerlichkeit* 17 (1982): 111–32.

"who we know loves us".[17] Her conversion consists ultimately in the fact that she was "freed from conversation as chatter with the world and about the world so as to enter into a real and essential conversation with God, about God, about herself, about people and her world as God sees them and from the perspective of God himself".[18] This most profound Being-in-dialogue, which can become a valid form of being human because it is the ontological form of the trinitarian God himself, opens a person anew to conversation with people as well. The chatter with which we so often greet one another is, after all, mostly a sublime sort of hide-and-go-seek; we talk about all sorts of things so as not to have to broach the subject of ourselves. Most of what Teresa wrote, considered purely in terms of its literary form, is not a literary composition for unknown future readers but, rather, a direct address to specific people, which proceeds from her direct address to God, leads into it, and often quite abruptly passes over into it, so that one interpreter could say: "Teresa's writings are a record of living speech with God and men."[19] Where the being of a person, as in Teresa's case, has become not only open, from its inmost foundation, but also a permanent act of Being-open toward the friend who is present, then there is dialogical existence in the authentic sense. Even in wordlessness this life is Being-addressed and Being-response. Contemplation is dialogue with the truth and gives to dialogue the breath of truth.

[17] Saint Teresa of Avila, *The Book of Her Life*, chap. 8, no. 5, in vol. 1 of *The Collected Works of St. Teresa of Avila*, trans. Kieran Kavanaugh, O.C.D., and Otilio Rodriguez, O.C.D. (Washington, D.C.: Institute of Carmelite Studies, 1976), 67: "For mental prayer in my opinion is nothing else than an intimate sharing between friends; it means taking time frequently to be alone with Him who we know loves us." Cf. Schiffers, "Unsinn einer Flucht vor Gott", 116.

[18] Schiffers, "Unsinn einer Flucht vor Gott", 115.

[19] Ibid.

2. Freedom

In this, however, freedom is realized. Today we are acquainted with a form of meditation in which religion becomes a drug. It is not concerned about a response to truth but rather about being freed from the burden and care of individual existence. It is about abandoning what is unbearable and leaden in everyday reality and experiencing instead the splendor of nothingness, the ontological heightening of the unreal. Although ostensibly its goal is to extinguish the self, to be free from one's ego, such religiosity is extremely selfish. It is not entering into a demanding relationship but, rather, allowing oneself to fall into the enjoyment of infinity. Karl Barth's warnings that religion could become the real antithesis of faith are become truly relevant today. The flight from faith into religion is part of the spiritual signature of the present day: the truth is too heavy, even though it may remain open, but its wonderful taste is what we want. Here the relations are reversed: even Orpheus looked around before he descended into the netherworld. Proper contemplation, like proper theory, searches for the truth without calculating its utility; here, though, the pleasant form is sought without wanting the trouble of the truth.

This, too, is one of the parodies of freedom with which we have to come to terms. For this illusory path of liberation leads only to illusion, and illusion is not freedom. Teresa's freedom—the freedom of someone who embarks on the dialogue of love and makes it the *logos* of her life—looks different. In Teresa's case, it is manifested in the two fundamental questions of her century: the question about the certainty of salvation and the question about works. To compare Teresa's answer to that of Luther would require a great deal of difficult hermeneutical mediation that I do not want to attempt here.[20] So I will simply present Teresa's answers as she gave them. For her, an objectifiable wish to be certain about one's own salvation is that sort of looking to oneself which kills the relationship on which salvation is based in the first place. Salvation is there only when I do not seek myself but, rather, remain oblivious to self in the act of encounter. We can find Teresa's position on this question summarized in two sentences from her work: "To beseech Him that we not offend Him is the greatest security we can have."[21] Our assurance is in looking to him and trusting in him, in giving ourselves freely. From there, the second thing can then be said: "In my opinion, it is impossible because of our nature for someone who doesn't know he is favored by God to have enthusiasm for great things."[22] One might translate *favorecido*: that God likes you, that you are in his good graces. This calm knowledge of being liked, of being accepted, which results from looking to him, has nothing to do with false assurance but everything to do with the freedom that provides the courage to act and to suffer.

Thus the completely and utterly non-quietist character of such contemplation becomes apparent. It is manifested even more clearly when Teresa puts it this way in another passage: "This is the reason for prayer, my daughters, the purpose of this spiritual marriage: the birth always of good works, good works."[23] Plainly an anxiously self-seeking piety of

[20] On this topic, see J. Moltmann, *Die Wendung zur Christusmystik bei Teresa von Avila*. Or: "Teresa von Avila und Martin Luther", *StdZ* 107 (1982): 449–63. The theme no doubt requires further discussion.

[21] *The Interior Castle*, The Seventh Dwelling Places, chap. 4, no. 3, in vol. 2 of the *Collected Works*, trans. Kieran Kavanaugh, O.C.D., and Otilio Rodriguez, O.C.D. (Washington, D.C.: Institute of Carmelite Studies, 1980), 445; Schiffers, "Unsinn einer Flucht vor Gott", 122.

[22] *Life*, chap. 10, no. 6, in *Collected Works* 1:76; Schiffers, "Unsinn einer Flucht vor Gott", 122.

[23] *The Interior Castle*, The Seventh Dwelling Places, chap. 4, no. 6, in

good works is not meant here. It does reject, however, a method of meditation that in the flight from self has self alone in mind: a kind of meditation that leaves the world to its own misery and is personally content to have found the way out. The contemplation of him who loved us to the point of folly does not lead to that sort of salvation-egotism but, rather, compels one to action and makes action the expression of the freedom from self that comes from the encounter with the truth and the redeeming power of its goodness.

3. *The truth*

All this has made it clear by now that Teresian mysticism is dialogical, that it is related to the truth and can never leave this dialogue behind. The new and previously unattainable feature is that now the truth is discovered as love—just as for Augustine the two fused into the recognition that the Logos can be no other than the crucified Christ, so that in him truth, love, and eternity fuse into one.[24] Faith, which in contemplation has become dialogue, is no longer understood as a dutiful assent to a lot of tenets. It loses all its external character. But it does not lose its content; it does not flee into the indefinite world of private experiences. The demanding and at the same time helpful thing about such dependence on the God who continues to confront me and addresses me in a very definite way becomes apparent in a sentence in which the entire faith perspective of this person, Teresa, becomes visible in the burden and grace of a life: "O infinite goodness of my God . . . ! How certainly You do suffer the one who suffers to be with

---

Collected Works 2:446; Schiffers, "Unsinn einer Flucht vor Gott", 122.
    [24] *Confessions* VII, 10, 16.

You!"[25] To put up with the truth, to put up with God—how difficult that can be! But ultimately the truth bears us up, because it is not a neuter thing but, rather, encounters us in him who bore all our burdens.

4. Worship

Finally, this dialogical orientation to liberating truth, which we recognize as the heart of Teresa's contemplation, acquires its specific form in her doctrine about remembering and thanking. First, remembering creates the context of a spiritual history in the individual person and at the same time brings history as a whole to him as his own history. Only remembering teaches understanding, makes a person grateful, and leads to love.[26] All this cannot be elaborated any further here. But one thing is clear anyway: with this teaching about remembrance and thanksgiving we have arrived at the heart of Christian worship, which in its most profound nature is nothing other than grateful remembrance and precisely thereby makes Plato's profound remark come true: that the ultimate meaning of all worship is that love might be made whole. The root of contemplation is worship; but worship needs contemplation if it is not to harden into ritualism. And only in this setting does that healing of the person come about which is neither flight nor violation but rather the dawn of the salvation we are all awaiting. Contemplation is the prerequisite for true action.

Last but not least, without trying to be ceremonious, I still have to wish the Catholic Academy in Bavaria, on this,

---

[25] *Life*, chap. 8, no. 6, in *Collected Works* 1:67; Schiffers, "Unsinn einer Flucht vor Gott", 124.

[26] Schiffers comments very beautifully on this, "Unsinn einer Flucht vor Gott", 127–31.

its anniversary, that it may continue to be an abode of the Muses, an abode of dialogue, a place of freedom that comes from the truth and is for the truth—all this supported by the faith-filled glorification of the one who is simultaneously saving love and liberating truth: Jesus Christ, our Lord.

The Catholic Academy in Bavaria had invited a small group to a forum on January 19, 2004, in which Professor Jürgen Habermas and Joseph Cardinal Ratzinger reflected on "The Pre-political Moral Foundations of a Free State". Within a few days, this encounter met with international acclaim that extended far into the Islamic world. Indeed, two outstanding representatives of quite different world views spoke with one another and reflected together on the fundamental question about the basis of human coexistence today: one of the most famous and influential contemporary philosophers, a proponent of secular liberal thought, and the Prefect of the Congregation for the Doctrine of the Faith, who at the same time is one of the most important theologians in the Church.

THE PRE-POLITICAL MORAL
FOUNDATIONS OF A FREE STATE

As the tempo of historical developments continues to accelerate around us, it seems to me that two factors are emerging as signs of a development that formerly proceeded only at a slow pace: on the one hand, the formation of a global society in which the individual political, economic, and cultural powers are increasingly interdependent and come into contact with one another in their different spheres of life and mutually interpenetrate. The other factor is the development of man's possibilities, of his power to make and to destroy, which raises the question of the legal and moral control of power in a way that goes far beyond anything customary until now. Thus it is a very urgent question, how cultures that encounter each other can find ethical foundations to guide their coexistence onto the right path and build a common, legally accountable structure that disciplines and orders power.

The fact that the "global ethic" project proposed by Hans Küng is in such demand shows in any case that the question has been framed. This is true even if one accepts the keen-sighted critique of this project that Robert Spaemann has offered.[1] For in addition to the two factors just mentioned,

---

Translated by Michael J. Miller.

[1] Robert Spaemann, "Weltethos als 'Projekt'", *Merkur* 570/571: 893–904.

there is a third: as cultures encountered and interpenetrated each other, the ethical certainties that had previously upheld society were to a great extent shattered in the process. The basic question of what is actually good now, especially in the given context, and why one must do it, even to one's own detriment, remains largely unanswered.

Now it seems obvious to me that science as such cannot produce ethics and that therefore a renewed ethical awareness cannot come about as the product of scientific debates. On the other hand, it is also indisputable that the fundamental change in our view of the world and of man that has resulted from the growth in scientific knowledge plays an essential part in the shattering of old moral certainties. In this respect, science does have a responsibility for man as man, and philosophy in particular has a responsibility to accompany critically the development of the individual sciences, to shed a critical light on hasty conclusions and pseudo-certainties about what man is, where he comes from, and why he exists, or, to put it another way, to eliminate the non-scientific element from the scientific findings with which it is often mixed and, thus, to keep our perspective open to the totality, to the broader dimensions of the reality of human existence, of which science can never manifest more than partial aspects.

Power and Law

Specifically, it is the task of politics to put power under the moderating influence of the law and thus to order the sensible use of it. Not the law of the stronger, but the strength of the law must prevail. Power that is ordered by law and at its service is the antithesis of violence, by which we understand lawless and unlawful power. That is why it is important for every society to overcome suspicion of the law and of its ordinances, because only thereby can arbitrariness be banished and freedom be experienced as a commonly shared freedom. Lawless freedom is anarchy and, therefore, the destruction of freedom. Suspicion of the law, rebellion against the law, will always spring up when the law itself appears, no longer as the expression of a justice that is at the service of all, but, rather, as the result of arbitrariness and legislative arrogance on the part of those who have power.

Hence the task of subjecting power to the criterion of law leads to the further question: How does law come into being, and how must law be constituted if it is to be a vehicle for justice and not the privilege of those who have the power to make the law? This poses, on the one hand, the question of the development of the law, but also, on the other hand, the question of its own intrinsic criteria. The law must not be an instrument of power wielded by a few but, rather, the expression of the common interest of all; this problem seems, initially at any rate, to be solved by the instruments of democratic consensus-building, because in them everyone collaborates in the development of the law and, hence, it is everyone's law and can and must be respected as such. In fact, the guarantee of common collaboration in shaping the law and in the just administration of power is the essential argument in favor of democracy as the most suitable form of political order.

Despite this, it seems to me, another question remains. Since it is difficult to find unanimity among men, nothing is left for democratic consensus-building but the indispensable instruments of delegated authority, on the one hand, and majority rule, on the other hand, in which varying percentages can be required for a majority depending on the importance of the issue. But even majorities can be blind or unjust. History demonstrates this all too clearly. When a majority, however large, puts down a minority—a religious or racial minority, for instance—by oppressive laws, can one still speak about justice or about law at all? Thus the majority principle still leaves open the question of the ethical foundations of the law, the question of whether something exists that can never become law and, therefore, something that always remains wrong in itself or, conversely, something that by its nature is unalterably right, that is, prior to any majority vote, and must be respected by it.

The modern era has formulated a set of such normative elements in various declarations of human rights and put them beyond the reach of shifting majorities. Nowadays one may be content with the intrinsically self-evident character of these values, given the contemporary awareness of their importance. But even such a self-limitation of the inquiry has a philosophical character. There are, therefore, self-subsistent values that follow from the nature of being human and, hence, are inviolable for all who possess this nature. We will have to return again later to the operational range of this idea, especially since its self-evident character is by no means recognized in all cultures. Islam has defined its own catalogue of human rights, which differs from the Western list. Although China today is defined by a form of culture, Marxism, that originated in the West, some have informed me that it nevertheless raises the question of whether human rights are not a typically Western invention that must be scrutinized.

Discussion with Professor Jürgen Habermas on "The Pre-political Moral Foundations of a Free State" during a forum at the Catholic Academy; January 19, 2004 (Photograph: Academy Archive).

New Forms of Power and
New Questions about Mastering It

In any discussion about the relation between power and law and about the sources of the law, a closer look must be taken at the phenomenon of power itself, also. Without trying to define the nature of power as such, I would like to sketch the challenges that result from the new forms of power that have developed in the last half century. The first phase of the period after World War II was dominated by alarm at the destructive power man had acquired with the invention of the atom bomb. Man suddenly saw himself in a position to destroy himself and the earth. This raised the question: What political mechanisms are necessary in order to ward off this destruction? How can such mechanisms be found and be made effective? How are we to mobilize the ethical forces that shape such political structures and make them work? Then, for a long period of time, it was de facto the competition between two opposing power blocs and the fear of bringing about one's own destruction with the destruction of the other that preserved us from the horrors of nuclear war. As it turned out, the reciprocal limitation of power and fear for one's own survival saved the day.

What makes us anxious these days is not so much fear of a large-scale war as fear of omnipresent terror that can strike and have its effect in any place. The human race, we see now, does not need a major war at all in order to make the world unlivable. The anonymous powers of terror, which can be present in all places, are strong enough to pursue everyone into the sphere of everyday life, whereby there is a lingering specter that criminal elements could gain access to weapons with great potential for destruction and thus deliver the world up to chaos apart from the political order. Thus the question about law and ethos has shifted: What are the sources on which terror feeds? How can this new sickness of mankind be eliminated successfully from within? The frightening thing about it is that terror, at least to some extent, claims moral legitimacy. Bin Laden's messages present terror as the response of the powerless, oppressed peoples to the haughtiness of the powerful, as the just punishment for their arrogance and for their blasphemous self-glorification and cruelty. For people in certain social and political situations, such motivations are evidently convincing. Sometimes terroristic behavior is depicted as the defense of religious tradition against the godlessness of Western society.

At this point a question arises, to which we must return later: If terrorism is fueled by religious fanaticism also— and it is—is religion then a healing, saving power, or is it not rather an archaic, dangerous power that sets up false, universalistic claims and thus leads astray to intolerance and terror? In that case, must not religion be placed under the guardianship of reason and be carefully restricted? Of course this also raises the question: Who can do that? How does one do that? But the general question remains: Should the gradual abolition of religion, the overcoming of religion, be regarded as necessary progress for mankind so that it can set out on the path of freedom and universal tolerance, or should it not?

Meanwhile, another form of power has come to the fore, which at first appears to be purely beneficent and thoroughly praiseworthy but in reality can lead to a new kind of threat to man. Man is now capable of making men, of growing them, so to speak, in a test tube. Man becomes a product, and with that the relation of man to himself is changed from top to bottom. He is no longer a gift of nature or of God the Creator; he is his own product. Man has descended into the springhouse of power, to the wellsprings of his own life. The temptation to construct man the right way at last, the temptation to experiment with men, the temptation to view men as garbage and to dispose of them, is not a mere figment of the imagination of some moralist opposed to progress.

Whereas earlier we considered the urgent question of whether religion really is a positive moral force, this now necessarily raises doubts about the reliability of reason. After all, the atom bomb, too, is ultimately a product of reason; ultimately the breeding and selection of men was devised by reason. Should not reason, therefore, in turn be placed under supervision now? But by whom or what? Or maybe religion and reason should limit each other reciprocally, each keeping the other within bounds and thus setting it on its positive path? At this juncture, the question again arises of how effective ethical clarity can be found in a global society with its mechanisms of power and with its unbridled forces as well as its different views of what constitutes law and morality: an ethics that has enough motivating force and persuasiveness to respond to the aforementioned challenges and to help deal with them.

Prerequisites for Law: Law—Nature—Reason

First this calls for a look at historical situations that are comparable to ours, to the extent that there is anything comparable. At any rate, it is worthwhile looking very briefly at the fact that ancient Greece had its own Enlightenment, that the divinely based law lost its self-evident character and an inquiry into the deeper justifications of law became necessary. And so the idea occurred to someone: In contrast to positive law, which can be unjust, there must be a law that follows logically from the nature, the being of man himself. This law must be found, and then it will serve as a corrective to positive law.

A less remote example is the twofold break for the European consciousness that occurred at the beginning of the modern era and compelled it to seek new bases for reflection on the content and source of law. First, there was the emergence from the confines of the European, Christian world that was accomplished with the discovery of America. Europeans were now encountering peoples who did not belong to the Christian system of faith and law, which until then had been the source of law for everyone and had shaped it. There was no law in common with those peoples. But were they then lawless, as many maintained at that time (and to a great extent acted accordingly), or is there a law that goes beyond all legal systems and unites and guides men as men in their relations to each other? In this situation, Francisco de Vitoria developed the idea of the *ius gentium*, the "law of the nations", which was already current, whereby the connotation of "heathens", "non-Christians", is implied by the word *gentes*. This meant, therefore, the law that is prior to the Christian legal structure and is supposed to arrange a just coexistence of all peoples.

The second break in the Christian world took place within Christendom itself through schism, through which the community of Christians was compartmentalized into opposing and sometimes hostile communities. Again, a common law that was prior to dogma, at least the minimal legal requirement, had to be developed, the foundations of which now had to lie, not in faith, but rather in the nature of man, in human reason. Hugo Grotius, Samuel von Pufendorf, and others developed the idea of natural law as a rational law that transcends confessional boundaries and establishes reason as the instrument of the common legislative project.

Natural law—especially in the Catholic Church—has remained the argumentative approach with which Christianity appeals to common reason in dialogues with secular society and with other faith communities and seeks the foundations for an agreement about the ethical principles of law in a secular, pluralistic society. But this instrument, unfortunately, has become dull, and therefore I would rather not rely on it in this discussion. The idea of natural law presupposes a concept of nature in which nature and reason mesh and nature itself is rational. This view of nature has collapsed with the victory of evolutionary theory. Nature as such is not rational, even though there is rational behavior in it: That is the diagnosis we hear from that camp, and today it seems to a large extent incontrovertible.[2] Thus, of the various dimensions of the concept of nature underlying the natural

[2] The philosophy of evolution, which is still dominant despite many corrections on individual points, is most impressively and consistently

law of former times, only one is left, which Ulpian (early third century A.D.) captured in the famous sentence: "Ius naturae est, quod natura omnia animalia docet" (The law of nature is what nature teaches all sentient beings).[3] But that very sentence is insufficient for our inquiries, which concern, not what is true of all *animalia*, but, rather, specifically human duties that man's reason has created and for which there could be no response without reason.

As the final element of the natural law, which at its deepest level intended to be a law of reason, in the modern era in any case, human rights have remained. They are not intelligible without the assumption that man as man, simply through his membership in the human species, is the subject of rights and that his very being bears within it values and norms

---

followed through in Jacques Monod, *Chance and Necessity: An Essay on the Natural Philosophy of Modern Biology* (New York, 1971). Helpful in distinguishing actual scientific findings from the accompanying philosophy is R. Junker and S. Scherer, eds., *Evolution: Ein kritisches Lehrbuch*, 4th ed. (Weyel, 1998). For references to the debate with the philosophy that accompanies the theory of evolution, see J. Ratzinger, *Truth and Tolerance: Christianity and World Religions*, trans. Henry Taylor (San Francisco: Ignatius Press, 2004), 162–83.

[3] On the three dimensions of medieval natural law (dynamic of being in general, the directedness of the nature common to human beings and animals [Ulpian], the specific directedness of man's rational nature), cf. the references in the article by P. Delhaye, "Naturrecht", in *LThK*, 2nd ed., 8:821–25. The concept of natural law found at the beginning of the *Decretum Gratiani* is noteworthy: "Humanum genus duobus regitur, naturali videlicet jure, et moribus. Ius naturale est, quod in lege et Evangelio continetur, quo quisque iubetur alii facere quod sibi vult fieri et prohibetur alii inferre quod sibi nolit fieri" (The human race is governed by two things, namely, natural law and customs. The natural law is the one contained in the Law and the Gospel, whereby everybody is commanded to do unto others what he wishes to be done to himself and is forbidden to inflict on others what he does not wish to be done to himself).

that are to be discovered but not invented. Perhaps today the doctrine of human rights ought to be supplemented by a doctrine of human duties and human limits, and that could now help to revive the question of whether there might not be a reason of nature and thus a rational law for man and his standing in the world. Today such a discussion would have to be designed and carried out at an intercultural level. For Christians, it would have to do with creation and the Creator. In the Indian world, the corresponding concept would be that of "dharma", the inner laws of being; and in the Chinese tradition, the idea of the ordinances of heaven.

Interculturality and Its Consequences

Before I try to draw conclusions, I would like to broaden a bit more the trail we have just blazed. Interculturality seems to me today to be an indispensable dimension for the discussion about the fundamental questions of human existence, which can be conducted neither as a merely intramural debate in Christianity nor merely within the Western rational tradition. In keeping with their self-understanding, both of these regard themselves as universal and may even be so de jure. De facto they must acknowledge that they are accepted only by parts of mankind and, furthermore, are comprehensible only in parts of mankind. The number of competing cultures is of course much smaller than it might seem at first glance.

The important thing, above all, is that there is no longer any uniformity within the cultural spheres; instead, all cultural spheres are characterized by far-reaching tensions within their own cultural tradition. In the West, this is quite obvious. Even though a strictly rational secular culture, of which Mr. Habermas gave us an impressive picture, is largely predominant and considers itself the element that binds people together, the Christian understanding of reality is now as ever an effective force. There are varying degrees of proximity or tension between the two poles; they may be willing to learn from each other or may have more or less decidedly rejected each other.

The Islamic cultural sphere, too, is characterized by similar tensions; there is a broad spectrum ranging from the fanatical absolutism of a Bin Laden to attitudes that are open to a tolerant rationality. The third great cultural sphere, Indian culture, or, more precisely, the cultural spheres of Hinduism and Buddhism, are again marked by similar tensions, even though they appear less dramatic, at least to our eyes. These cultures, too, find that they are exposed to the claim of Western rationality and also to the inquiries of the Christian faith, which are both present within them; they assimilate the one and the other in different ways while seeking to maintain their own identity. The tribal cultures of Africa and the tribal cultures of Latin American that have been reawakened by certain Christian theologies complete the picture. They appear to a great extent to call Western rationality into question but also to question the universal claim of Christian revelation.

What can we conclude from all this? First, it seems to me, the two great cultures of the West, the culture of Christian faith and that of secular rationality, are in fact not universal, however influential they both may be, each in its own way, throughout the world and in all cultures. In this respect, the question of the colleague from Teheran mentioned by Mr. Habermas seems to me to be of some importance, after all: namely, the question of whether the sociology of religion and a comparative study of cultures might not suggest that European secularization is an exceptional path in need of correction. I would not unconditionally, at least not necessarily, reduce this question to the state of mind of Carl Schmitt, Martin Heidegger, and Lévi-Strauss—that of a European situation weary of rationality, so to speak. The fact is, in any case, that our secular rationality, however obvious it is to our Western-trained reason, does not make sense to every *ratio* and that in its attempt to make itself evident, as rationality, it runs into its limitations. Its self-evidence is in fact bound up with definite cultural contexts, and, that being the case, it must acknowledge that it cannot be reproduced in mankind as a whole and, hence, cannot be wholly operative in it, either. In other words, the rational or the ethical or the religious formula of the world on which everyone agreed and which then could support the whole does not exist. In any case, it is presently unattainable. That is why even the so-called world ethic remains an abstraction.

Conclusions

What is to be done, then? With regard to the practical consequences, I find myself largely in agreement with the remarks of Mr. Habermas about a post-secular society and about a willingness to learn and self-limitation on both sides. To conclude this lecture, I would like to summarize my own view in two theses.

1. We have seen that there are pathologies in religion that are extremely dangerous and that make it necessary to regard the divine light of reason, so to speak, as a regulatory body; religion must again and again be purified and ordered anew in terms of reason—which, incidentally, was also the idea of the Church Fathers.[4] But our reflections also showed that,

---

[4] I tried to describe this in more detail in my book *Truth and Tolerance*, which was mentioned in n. 2; cf. also M. Fiedrowicz, *Apologie im frühen Christentum*, 2nd ed. (Schöningh, 2001).

although mankind in general is not as aware of it, there are also pathologies of reason, a *hubris* of reason that is no less dangerous but even more menacing in terms of its potential efficiency: atom bomb, man as product. That is why, conversely, reason, too, must be reminded about its limits and must learn to be willing to listen to the great religious traditions of mankind. If it completely emancipates itself and rejects this willingness to learn and this correlative status, it becomes destructive.

Kurt Hübner recently formulated a similar demand and said that such a thesis does not directly involve a "return to faith" but, rather, is a matter of "being liberated from the momentous delusion that it (that is, faith) has nothing more to say to contemporary man because it contradicts one's humanistic idea of reason, enlightenment, and freedom."[5] Accordingly, I would speak about a necessary relatedness between reason and faith, reason and religion, which are called to purify and heal each other; they need each other and must recognize each other.

2. This basic rule must then find concrete expression in practice, in the intercultural context of the present day. No doubt the two main partners in this mutual relatedness are Christian faith and Western secular rationality. This can and must be said without any false Euro-centrism. The two determine the world situation to an extent unequalled by any other cultural force. But that does not mean that one could set the other cultures aside as a sort of "negligible quantity". That would indeed be a sort of Western *hubris*, and we would pay dearly for it—to some extent we are already paying the price. It is important for these two major components of Western culture to assume an attitude of listen-

[5] K. Hübner, *Das Christentum im Wettstreit der Religionen* (Mohr Siebeck, 2003), 148.

ing and to enter into a true relatedness with these cultures as well. It is important to include them in the attempt at a polyphonic relatedness, in which they open themselves to the essential complementariness of reason and faith, so that a universal process of purifications can develop, in which the essential values and norms that are somehow known or sensed by all men can finally gain new illuminating power, so that what holds the world together can again become an effective force in mankind.

The Romano Guardini Prize for 1982 is awarded to Mother Gemma Hinricher, O.C.D., at the annual celebration and the Silver Jubilee of the Catholic Academy in Bavaria; June 27, 1982 (Photograph: Academy Archive/Gerd Pfeiffer).

Tributes

At its anniversary celebration in Munich on March 14, 1978, the Catholic Academy in Bavaria awarded the Romano Guardini Prize to the Bavarian Prime Minister at that time, Alfons Goppel. Presenting this award, which since 1970 has been conferred for "outstanding services in interpreting the times and the world in all areas of the intellectual life", was Joseph Cardinal Ratzinger, as President of the Bavarian Conference of Bishops and also as Regent of the Academy. In his tribute, he described the deeply Christian, markedly Catholic personality of Alfons Goppel sympathetically and vividly. Furthermore, he combined this eulogy with an attempt to situate political activity prompted by a Christian sense of responsibility within the larger context of shaping the world as the philosopher of religion Romano Guardini understood it.

COMMENDATION OF PRIME
MINISTER ALFONS GOPPEL

Recipient of the 1978 Romano Guardini Prize

Anyone who lines up the recipients of the Romano Guardini Prize side by side will at first be surprised above all by
the breadth and range of this prize. The series starts with
two theologians who understood theology as an inquiry
into the whole of reality and pursued it as a responsibility
to the whole world that is entrusted to us: Karl Rahner and
Hans Urs von Balthasar. At the end, there are two politi-
cians: Teddy Kollek, the Mayor of Jerusalem, and Alfons
Goppel, who for almost sixteen years has been Prime Minister of the Free State of Bavaria. Many people who understand Guardini's work primarily in aesthetic and literary
terms may wonder whether the idea of "interpreting the
world", which is the criterion for the prize, may not have
been precariously overextended.

That very term "aesthetic" might be able to help us here:
Guardini was certainly no aesthetician, much less an aes-
theticist, as he is sometimes accused of being. But he was,
by all means, a man with an artist's intuition, which opened
up for his thinking horizons that remain hidden from the
academic specialist when he pursues scholarship merely as
the craft of the verifiable. Because this is so, it is only right
that one of the series of prize winners should be a Bavarian

Translated by Michael J. Miller.

artist of European renown: Carl Orff. When the Bundes-
verdienstkreuz [an order of merit awarded by the German
Federal Republic] was conferred on Orff in June 1965, Alfons Goppel described his work in a way that shows briefly
yet evocatively how the musician Orff is an interpreter of
the world: "Thus he leads [the listener] back to the heart of
human thought: to the active, playing, and singing configu-
ration of life's course, which shows the truth of existence in
the semblance of the theatrical world, the intellectuality that
connects feeling and thinking in the sound and rhythm of
language and song, and the unalterable, God-given laws of
being in the context of the joy and sorrow of all liveliness."[1]
On that occasion Goppel applied to Orff what Orff had formerly said about Hindemith: "Hindemith stood completely
within his time. He knew about the time and confronted it as
scarcely anyone else did. He never refused an answer, and he
spared himself no challenge. He was formed and supported
by it, until finally, as though he had outgrown the time, he
made his mark on it with the utmost self-assurance."[2] I think
that this is a statement that we can now impart once again,
one that may be applied also to the lifelong accomplishment
of Alfons Goppel, since it points out his relationship to the
time and his significance for the time.

Politics as Art

The artist as interpreter of the world—anyone who says
this, and does so in connection with two different and yet
by all means related Guardini prizewinners, will recall that

---

[1] A. Goppel, *Reden: Ausgewählte Manuskripte aus den Jahren 1958–1965*
(Würzburg, n.d.), 130.

[2] Ibid., 129.

Plato understood politics as art and thereby at the same time set a standard for politics. The most significant discussion of this is found in the dialogue *Gorgias*, which, because of its relentless confrontation with the sophistical destruction of language, of man, and of the State, stands in almost uncanny proximity to the problems that beset us today. Plato's Socrates speaks there about the two arts that exist: "The one that pertains to the soul I call politics", while the one pertaining to the body he calls gymnastics and medicine. In each case, however, he mentions also the pseudo-art that dons the mantle of the real one and thus ruins everything. The distinctive feature of pseudo-art is that it strives for what is pleasant while excluding what is best; together with the pleasant, it chases after stupidity and deceives it. While searching for the boundary line with seductive pseudo-art, which defrauds man of the good by means of the pleasant, Plato finds the clarification of what he calls art and discovers in what way true politics is "art" in his view: Pseudo-art, the capacity (which is often taken to a devilish degree of refinement) to gain power and to bind people to oneself with the convenience of untruth, is nevertheless not an "art" but, rather, only an "experience", ἐμπειρία. It is so because it is "unable to explain or to give a reason": "I do not call any irrational thing an art."[3] Accordingly, art, from Plato's perspective, is the shaping of reality that occurs based on knowledge about reason and with a responsibility to reason. Aristotle formulated it as follows: Art is the capacity to work formatively in terms of the correct meaning.[4] Aristotle, who

---

[3] *Gorgias* 465a, from *The Dialogues of Plato*, trans. Benjamin Jowett, vol. 2 (New York: Macmillan & Co., 1892), 346. The current relevance of *Gorgias* is spelled out strikingly by J. Pieper, *Kümmert euch nicht um Sokrates: Drei Fernsehspiele* (Munich, 1966), 11–80.

[4] *Nicomachean Ethics* VI, 4, 1140a 9f. F. Dirlmeier, in his *Aristoteles,*

attempts to order concepts, adds that the substance of politics is, not making but, rather, acting responsibly; in this respect, he prefers to call it a science, or *dynamis*, without simply refusing to give it the name "art".[5]

In a speech that he gave in 1965 at the statewide meeting of the *Junge Union* [the joint youth organization of the Christian Democratic Union and Christian Social Union, two political parties in Germany], Alfons Goppel identified freedom, personal responsibility, and human dignity as the leading ideas of his politics, which therefore "do not have to be reformulated again and again in endless discussions or lofty declamations, because they are deeply embedded in the Christian world view, without which the Western concept of freedom and humanity could not have set out on its triumphant progress over the whole world."[6] In his address at the installation of the founding rector of the University of Regensburg, he referred to the founding of all education and, thus, of every political community, too, through formation in the family, which in turn is dependent "on those powers for living that have been placed by nature in our hearts and minds, namely, that reverence for God and intellect, for life and living, and that humility toward what is great and shared in common."[7] In other words, the best heritage

---

Nikomachische Ethik (Darmstadt, 1956), translates μετά λόγου ἀληθοῦς, which I have rendered "von der richtigen Sinngebung her" (in terms of the correct meaning), as "von richtigem Reflektieren geleitet" (derived from correct reflection) (p. 126). In any case, it means behavior that is supported by thought that understands meaning.

[5] Politics as δύναμις: *Magna Moralia* I, 1, 1182b 1f. On the connection between τέχνη and δύναμις, see *Prior Analytics* 30, 46 a 22; *Metaphysics* I, 1, 981 a 3; *Nicomachean Ethics* I, 1, 1094 a 7 (connection of τέχνη and ἐπιστήμη), et passim.

[6] *Reden*, 26.

[7] Ibid., 110.

from the sources of Western tradition: from the intellectual achievement of Greece and its creative humanity, from the spirit of the Christian faith and its reverence for the dignity of man, who has been created and called by God. Politics in this spirit is more than mere ἐμπειρία—routine skill in making, without knowledge of the meaning on which it is based. Politics is interpretation of the world in terms of its reason; it allows us to understand again Plato's saying, which had become so foreign, that politics has something to do with soul and therefore is the central art, the decisive form of interpreting the world.

Bajuwarität—Being Bavarian

In the remarks by Alfons Goppel just cited, we do not hear a political program, but we do see something of his own personality. In attempting to describe it, I feel compelled once more to borrow lines from Goppel's speech about Carl Orff. "No tribute", it says there, "can overlook one fundamental fact: his *Bajuwarität* (Bavarianness)", which Goppel then characterizes more precisely as a combination of earthy humanity and transcendental relatedness.[8] *Bajuwarität*—in Alfons Goppel, too, being Bavarian means just this: delight in the earth, in the home, the world, and in life, a cheerfulness that even in the perplexities of ominous times does not cease to recognize that this world was created good by God and to rejoice in that. Combined with this is an unsentimental religiosity that does not make the world ascetically gloomy but, rather, illuminates and brightens it with the faith. *Bajuwarität*—for Alfons Goppel this means simultaneously a German, a European, and a cosmopolitan attitude.

[8] Ibid., 128.

Conversing with Alfons Goppel, the Bavarian Prime Minister, during the reception at the Catholic Academy following the episcopal ordination of Joseph Ratzinger; May 28, 1977 (Photograph: Academy Archive/Gerd Pfeiffer).

His birthplace, the old imperial city of Regensburg, and his heritage—his mother, who came from the Upper Palatinate, and his Swabian father—set for him a standard of open-mindedness that was borne out by his career: he spent a good part of his life in Frankish Aschaffenburg and thus came to know and love the land of the Franks along with greater Bavaria; he took a wife from the Westphalian town of Bentheim on the Dutch border; they met, of course, beside a well at the University of Munich, in an almost biblical way, then, since Scripture tells of how Moses and Isaac, too, found their wives at the well, that primordial place of human encounters. Wherever Alfons Goppel is honored and praised, his wife, Gertrud, must also be gratefully honored and praised: the humanity that radiates from her, the womanly and motherly warmth that emanates from her, are an indispensable part of the Goppel era. The Bavarian experience as Alfons and Gertrud Goppel live it has nothing to do with stubborn insistence on one's own limited views; it comes completely into its own only and precisely through openness to the world, through a German and European attitude.

Responsibility for the Land

Corresponding to the geographical radius within which the life of Alfons Goppel has moved is the span of time that extends from the era of the Prince Regent Luitpold through the Weimar Republic, the Third Reich, and the years of the world wars and into the atomic age. Goppel's father was secretary of the Christian Labor Union. Alfons, the fourth of nine children, knew and knows, not just from books but from his own experience, what poverty and deprivation mean. But when he speaks about his upbringing and his parents' home in his speech at the University of Regensburg, he likewise knows what he is talking about: a heritage, his "roots", which even today continue to nourish his life. His first foray into politics, a seat as a city councilman in Regensburg that he won in the last free elections in 1933, was cut short by the tyranny of National Socialism, which sent the freely elected men back home. After the inferno of the war, the impulse to do political work became virtually imperative for Goppel: Anyone who has lived through that, he explained, *must* assume political responsibility, so that the same thing cannot happen again. Responsibility for the land and for people, the conviction of his Christian conscience, was the point of departure for the political career of the man who for the last almost sixteen years has been the Bavarian Prime Minister. In this tribute to the Guardini Prize recipient, I do not need to describe the individual stages of Goppel's political path or depict the crucial points of his work in government. The fact that Bavaria has assumed a new face during his administration and in so doing has remained true to itself can be shown in a few words. During Goppel's terms of office, five new state universities were founded: Regensburg, Augsburg, Bayreuth, Passau, and also the comprehensive university in Bamberg; he also energetically promoted the construction and expansion of the Church-affiliated University of Eichstätt. The years of Goppel's administration saw the reconstruction of the National Theater and the Residence [historic castle and former residence of Bavarian nobility in the capital, Munich]. Under Goppel, Bavaria has become a modern industrial region, which today occupies a significant position in the economy of the Federal Republic of Germany. Goppel, however, was also the first head of government to set up a ministry for land development and environmental issues, thus charting a new course for the future at a time when the ideology of economic growth was still predominant and almost unchecked. Similarly, the Goppel era saw the establishment of the Bavarian Forest National Park, the environmental protection law, and the law for the preservation of monuments—all of them legislative projects in which Bavaria took a leading role in meeting the new demands of our time. It is in keeping with Goppel's European and cosmopolitan attitude that he conspicuously carried out initiatives that crossed borders as well and brought Bavaria's international status to bear: he collaborated substantially in the founding of the Association of Alpine States, and he also put into political action what he declared in 1965 in a speech to the statewide assembly of the Christian-Social Union in Munich: "Bavaria", he had said on that occasion, "is something like the railway turntable leading to southeastern Europe."[9] Six months before that, in his speech at the University of Regensburg, he had spoken about the Danube as the way leading to the southeast and thus interpreted the river as a signpost and a mission.[10] As a final link in this chain of achievements in foreign policy matters, we all vividly recall the Bavarian exhibition in Moscow and Goppel's visit with the premier of the Soviet Union, which show that a decisive and clear debate with Marxism by no means has to stand in the way of a policy of peace and productive encounters.

Truth and Conscience

Let us return once again to Plato's *Gorgias*, which set up the image of true politics as an art at the service of souls at a time

[9] Ibid., 9.
[10] Ibid., 111.

of profound peril to the State and thus to souls, also. This peril, according to Plato's diagnosis, was based on skill at using words without responsibility to the truth and at deluding men with the pleasant and thus leading them away from the good. Plato's Socrates says in this connection that the "rhetoricians", that is, the experts at words without responsibility to the truth, "are . . . like tyrants; . . . they kill and despoil and exile any one they please."[11] In Germany, we have experienced the tyrant who kills, exiles, and despoils. Plato in his time, when apparently there was no tyrant in sight, had to warn that the reckless use of words is a tyranny of its own sort, which in its way likewise kills, despoils, and exiles. Certainly there are today, too, plenty of reasons to express similar warnings and to call up the forces that are capable of arresting such tyranny, which is noticeably in the ascendant. The experience of Hitler's bloody tyranny and an alertness to new dangers were what made Romano Guardini become in his later years, almost despite his temperament, a dramatic herald warning against the corruption of politics through its detachment from conscience and brought him to the point of calling on the man who acts politically out of faith for a correct, not merely theoretical but real, active interpretation of the world. "The unbeliever is not in a position to manage the world correctly", he says in one of these speeches.

> Forces that would be strong enough to keep one's own power in order come neither from science nor from technology itself. But neither do they come from an autonomous ethic of the individual, much less from some sovereign wisdom of the State. . . . The truly saving possibilities lie within the conscience of the man who is in a

[11] *Gorgias* 466c–d, p. 348.

living union with God. . . . Perhaps someday the preservation of the world will depend in the most elementary sense on whether the Christian takes responsibility for it.[12]

These sentences of that great Christian scholar unmistakably converge with words that the politician Goppel formulated —as his personal affirmation as well—at the foundation of the University of Regensburg: "Always and everywhere, how decisions are made will depend, not on knowledge, but rather on conscience, which is of course formed and guided by it."[13] Even Goppel's political opponents do not dispute the fact that the standard of his politics has always remained ultimately the responsibility of a well-formed Christian conscience; this is also the reason why he has political opponents but no enemies. To be grateful for this kind of political activity and its interpretation of the world is profoundly in keeping with Romano Guardini's legacy. And so I heartily congratulate this year's Guardini Prize recipient: the sovereign father of our land, Alfons Goppel.

[12] R. Guardini, *Sorge um den Menschen* (Würzburg, 1962), 83f., 85. Cf. *Gebet und Wahrheit: Meditationen über das Vaterunser* (Würzburg, 1960), 184f.; translated by Isabel McHugh as *The Lord's Prayer* (Sophia Institute Press, 1996). See also his famous essay from the year 1946: "Der Heilbringer in Mythos, Offenbarung und Politik", in R. Guardini, *Unterscheidung des Christlichen: Gesammelte Studien 1923–1963*, 2nd ed. (Mainz, 1963), 411–56. See also H. U. von Balthasar, *Romano Guardini: Reform from the Source*, trans. Albert K. Wimmer and D. C. Schindler (Communio; San Francisco: Ignatius Press, 2010), esp. 21ff.

[13] *Reden*, 110.

On the occasion of the one hundredth birthday of Romano Guardini (February 17, 1885–October 1, 1968), the Catholic Academy in Bavaria, which is greatly indebted to the work of that philosopher of religion, theologian, literary critic, and educator, organized a festive colloquium in Munich on February 2, 1985. During this well-attended event, the speakers investigated selected aspects of his work, in particular the question of why Guardini's specific approach, which goes beyond mere "scholarship", to this day is able to provide answers to those seeking existential guidance from the Christian faith. The final lecture, which is reprinted here, made this connection also: Joseph Cardinal Ratzinger gave an incisive evaluation of Romano Guardini's theology and in doing so went far beyond the parameters of a merely pious, retrospective commemorative address.

FROM LITURGY TO CHRISTOLOGY

Romano Guardini's Basic Theological
Approach and Its Significance

Birthday speeches are dangerous. They can easily become a closing refrain, words of praise that often scarcely conceal the underlying farewell to what is irrevocably past. What are we doing, then, when we celebrate Romano Guardini's hundredth birthday? Is this just the nostalgia of those whose encounter with Guardini became a formative intellectual experience and who would like to share what was valuable to them with the younger generation but forget that a new time demands new guides? Or is Romano Guardini a voice of the present, also, which we merely have to make audible again? Or perhaps the two alternatives are by no means so mutually exclusive as they appear at first glance. For when someone has not only written books but was once able to make a lively impression on a whole generation, then this in itself is already something of a lasting achievement. And, conversely, no one can continue to exert influence through written works alone but can do so only through living mediators who discover the present relevance in a word from the past and are able to see it and live it anew. Every human utterance is situated in its time and carries within it the limitations of an age. The question is whether such words are backed up by the experience and suffering of humanity, of reality itself, which touch the core of our being and

Translated by Michael J. Miller.

therefore can once more awaken new experience and new understanding. The so-called timeless qualities are not what counts about an author. The supposedly timeless extract that many interpreters distill from philosophers and theologians of the past and offer to their readers as something lasting has always been for me the most boring part, because all that remained was banal and insignificant. The more forcefully a man confronts his time and meets the demands of humanity in it, the more valid his message will continue to be, even though it can be experienced only by way of an encounter with what for me is initially something or someone different. Only when we allow ourselves to be touched by what is truly other do we come into our own. The time when Guardini was simply one of us and spoke to us in the voice of the immediate present is ineluctably slipping away. The question is whether the otherness into which he is departing for the time being carries within it the force of the encounter that can bring him before us again and bring us to ourselves.

I. The Liturgical Awakening and Its Place in the Philosophy of History

Let us take a look and not hesitate to seize valiantly this otherness, wherever it is found. For it is undoubtedly there. In Guardini's early liturgical writings what strikes us as odd is not only the linguistic pathos, the romanticism of youth setting out for new and distant shores. What is actually different, indeed, strange, lies in the view of history on which this pathos feeds. One of the characteristic sentences from *Liturgische Bildung* (Liturgical formation)[1] reads: "The 'mod-

---

[1] Romano Guardini, *Liturgische Bildung: Versuche* (Rothenfels, 1923), 26.

ern era' is past—we hope that it is!" Here he sets the basic tone of hope and confidence in a new era (after long years of erring) to which the whole book is tuned. What is now beginning seems like the shattering of a long illusion; now finally the land of the future lies open and free again, in which a new youth movement is advancing so as to build a better world. It is understandable that precisely this confidence of the early-morning hour, the sense of escape from old associations, was able to inspire young people and won a hearing for the voice of the man who spoke that way. "The 'modern era' is past—we hope that it is!" For Guardini "the end of the modern era" was not just some theoretical idea from the philosophy of history; rather, it was an existential experience, an awakening from the twilight of his own early-morning beginning, together with other young people who understood him and whose understanding gave him an awareness of his own calling and special mission. The modern era was for Guardini the disintegration of man, of the world in general, into a mere intellectuality, which thereby becomes "mendacious", and a mere materiality, which is only the instrument of human projects. In his opinion, the modern era was striving for pure intellectuality, "and what happened was one of the most terrible mistakes ever to avenge a defection from the substantial outlook: they wanted what was purely intellectual and ended up in the abstract."[2] But now, he maintained, we see with horror how thoroughly and utterly unspiritual this world was, "how terribly dead: namely, the world of concepts, formulas, apparatuses, mechanisms, and organizations".[3] At the same time, the departure of such mendacious intellectuality means: "Away from the brutish materiality of the same century, which so unnaturally enjoyed being descended from an

[2] Ibid., 23.
[3] Ibid., 24.

animal!"[4] Turning away from the modern era is combined in the young Guardini with a new, almost rapturous enthusiasm for the medieval period, as it looked at him out of P. L. Landsberg's book *Das Mittelalter und wir* [The Middle Ages and us] (Bonn, 1923), which evidently had become for him a sort of key reading experience.[5]

Guardini's liturgical idea is initially situated completely within this context: to rediscover the liturgy is to rediscover the unity of soul and body in the wholeness of one man, for liturgical behavior is corporeal-spiritual behavior, an emergence from a piety that had been narrowed down to merely spiritual and psychological elements into a prayer that in its corporeal and communal action is the unity of all reality. Consequently, liturgical action is more specifically symbolic action that is capable of grasping the world and its own being as symbol, because the symbol is the real epitome of the unity of spirit and the matter, the spirituality of matter and the materiality of the spiritual. Where the two break apart, the symbol is lost, and the capacity for liturgy ends, also, because the world is split dualisti-

[4] Ibid., 26f.

[5] Cf. the reference in Guardini's lecture "Anselm von Canterbury und das Wesen der Theologie", in *Auf dem Wege: Versuche* (Mainz, 1923), in which Guardini—as he does repeatedly in other writings of the same period—cites Landsberg's book and adds the comment, "In recent years not much has been published that I could compare with this work" (p. 45, n. 1). On Guardini's relationship to Landsberg, see H.-B. Gerl, *Romano Guardini, 1885–1968: Leben und Werk* (Mainz, 1985), 130f. and 142. Meanwhile, Guardini made every effort not to lapse into a romanticism of the medieval; see, for example, *Liturgische Bildung* 52, n. 2: "Although the Middle Ages are accentuated here and it is shown in what ways they were superior to the modern era, this is no romanticism. I neither think that the modern era is bad . . . ; nor do I demand that our time should imitate the Middle Ages. . . . Every age has its mission. . . . Every age should and can be Catholic. . . . I think that Ranke said it: Not imitation, but rather self-examination and self-discovery."

cally into mind and body, subject and object. But if the authentic self-actualization of Christianity is liturgical action, if its central way of understanding reality is presented in the symbol, then what is at stake in the struggle for symbol and liturgy is man realizing his fundamental essence—one of Guardini's favorite expressions.[6] It follows that the question of overcoming the modern era touched the heart of his thought, no, of his whole personal existence as a man and as a Christian.

The whole thing returns once again—without any change in the basic orientation yet taken farther into a new vision —in one of Guardini's last statements about the liturgical question, in the letter he wrote in 1964 to a participant in the third liturgical congress in Mainz. There we find the famous question that, in the midst of the euphoria of the Second Vatican Council's liturgical reform, revealed quite severely the core of the real effort and its ultimate human depth: "Is the liturgical act, and with it what we call 'liturgy' in the first place, so bound up with history—antiquity or the Middle Ages—that to be honest one would have to give it up entirely?"[7] At the time, Guardini's question was turned into an

---

[6] Cf. *Liturgische Bildung*, 22ff.; *The Spirit of the Liturgy*, translated by Ada Lane (New York: Crossroad Publications, 1998), 61–72, esp. 69.

[7] *Liturgie und liturgische Bildung* (Würzburg, 1966), 16. Substantially the same question—only formulated in more general terms—can be found in its entirety in *Religion und Offenbarung* (Würzburg, 1958), 105: "The image of the world is progressively losing its religious dimension; it is becoming more profane. . . . As a result, religious behavior loses its self-evident character. It increasingly becomes a task . . . with constantly growing demands. This gives rise to the question of whether the process can continue so far that religious behavior in general will disappear or perhaps withdraw into vestigial forms. If one imagines, for instance, the endeavors in atheistic, totalitarian countries continuing over a longer period of time and with ever more systematic methods, the question can become very distressing."

opinion poll,[8] but that is precisely what he did not intend. For him it was not a question about new tactics, perhaps because one tactic that had just been devised and ultimately accepted seemed to be getting dull again right at the outset. What he intended was a fundamental question about man and his potential for belief, in which we hear something of the obscurity of Jesus' question: "Nevertheless, when the Son of man comes, will he find faith on earth?" (Lk 18:8). Guardini had run out of the optimistic pathos of his earlier hour; the fact that man is soul in body, body in soul, and that liturgy and symbol therefore bring him to what is essential in himself—he had not come to doubt that. He wondered, rather, how radical the alienation of man in history could someday become.

Guardini did not retract the thesis about the end of the modern era, either, although the post-modern era certainly presented very early on a completely different face from the one he thought he could perceive in the initial hour of the awakening. Although Guardini's early lectures are still entirely characterized by the confidence of a new beginning, of an epochal turning point, the same year 1923 in which *Liturgische Bildung* once again showed flashes of the lofty optimism of the beginning brought him already an experience of an entirely different sort. The letters from Lake Como reflect the shock that Guardini felt at the intrusion of technological civilization into the landscape of Southern Europe and its great urban culture. From then on, the picture becomes more melancholy, and the diagnoses become harsher, even though he holds on to that hope that, with almost palpable pain and sorrow, is formulated in the sentences from *The End of the Modern World* that have become classic: "A fullness of religious sensibility helps faith, but it can also veil

---

[8] Cf. the comments by the editors (J. Messerschmid and H. Waltmann) in *Liturgie und liturgische Bildung*, 17f., n. 1.

and secularize its content. If this fullness diminishes, faith becomes leaner but purer and stronger . . . with decision, loyalty and self-conquest."[9] Of course this hope became increasingly more difficult for Guardini; the endangerment of

[9] *The End of the Modern World*, trans. Elinor C. Briefs (Wilmington, Del.: Intercollegiate Studies Institute, 1998), 113. A first hint at a critical view can be found perhaps already in the *Liturgische Bildung* (Spring 1923). Granted, a fundamental emotional tone of confidence prevails; besides the passages mentioned at the outset, see p. 42 in particular: "A turn of events has started"; p. 70: "But we feel that here, too, the turn has started." Thus Guardini stays along the lines of the works composed in 1916–1921, which he published (likewise in 1923) in the little anthology *Auf dem Wege: Versuche*. In *Liturgische Bildung*, at any rate, we find this remark: "Our era is marching from an individualistic yesterday into a perhaps communist tomorrow. Both are far from true community" (78). But this just remains a theoretical consideration. The culture shock that really penetrates deep into his soul occurred in 1923 at Lake Como: "We are used to it in the North. We have even learned to see something valuable in what is unavoidable. . . . But see, here it was totally different! Here was form closer to humanity. Here was nature indwelt by humanity. And now I saw it breaking apart. I thus became aware of what I had not been [aware of] in the North, because previously I had become accustomed to such things. The world of natural humanity . . . was perishing! I cannot tell you how sad this made me" (*Letters from Lake Como: Explorations in Technology and the Human Race*, trans. Geoffrey W. Bromiley [Grand Rapids: Eerdmans, 1994], 7). The final letter attempts to find a positive side to this analysis, which H. U. von Balthasar called "heartrending" (*Romano Guardini*, 12): "Our place is in what is evolving. We must take our place, each at the right point. We must not oppose what is new and try to preserve a beautiful world that is inevitably perishing. . . . We must transform what is coming to be. But we can do this only if we honestly say yes to it. . . . Our age has been given to us as the soil on which we stand and the task to master. At bottom we do not wish it otherwise" (80–81). This tension between the grief of loss and the confidence in transformation then remained Guardini's position, which he classically formulated in *The End of the Modern World*. The rightly debated formula "the end of the modern world" is clearly rooted, however, in the deliberations of the *Liturgische Bildung*, where it has another quite positive meaning and also an inner logic, which was

the religious act in the secondary world of self-made objects affected him more and more deeply.

Something of the gravity of the late hour hangs over the 1964 letter, despite all the joy over the liturgical reform of the Council that grew out of his work. A summons to attempt new and bolder liturgical experiments that would lead to the destruction of what was originally intended—the objectivity, positivity, historical wealth, and ecclesiality of the liturgy—was surely not the aim of his questioning. On the contrary, he was concerned about a return to what is authentic, what is "essential": Guardini summons the liturgists gathered in Mainz to take seriously the alienation of those who consider the liturgy to be no longer comprehensible and to reflect on "how—if the liturgy is essential—one can approach them".[10] Precisely by the restraint of the verbal expression, the letter had intended to emphasize the fact that he himself did not doubt for one second that it was indispensable and that therefore *this* question ought to be posed categorically. In retrospect, one can only regret that people allowed this large question to sink to the level of a banal opinion poll instead of making it the inner guiding principle of the reform effort.

With that we have now got ahead of ourselves, though, because it became evident what part of the pathos of the 1920s, Guardini himself was able to cast off and where this extremely time-bound pathos still directly touches the nerve

---

lost, though, in the transition to the perspective of cultural critique. A concise presentation of Guardini's analysis of the times can be found in Von Balthasar, *Romano Guardini*, 9–19; cf. also Gerl, *Romano Guardini*, 338–42, and especially the penetrating study by J. H. Schmucker-von Koch, *Autonomie und Transzendenz* (Mainz, 1985), as well as the remarks in E. Biser, "Romano Guardini: Wegweiser in eine neue Epoche", in W. Seidel, ed., *Christliche Weltanschauung: Wiederbegegnung mit Romano Guardini* (Würzburg, 1985), 210–40.

[10] *Liturgie und liturgische Bildung*, 17.

of Christian and human existence in general. But it may still
be useful, before we proceed, to explain again briefly how
far removed that pathos in fact is for the moment from today's historical consciousness. It so happened that, just as I
began to read Guardini intensively again, I had to complete a
rather long essay for the recently published *Nuovo dizionario
di liturgia* (Rome, 1984), in which I found precisely the opposite assessments: The liturgy, the writer claimed, is certainly threatened from outside as well by the pressure to secularize, but it is threatened chiefly by the existing form of
Christian experience in the Church, which became set in the
Middle Ages. Despite the efforts of Vatican II, it is difficult
for her to detach herself from it and to be open to change.[11]
The author then reaches even farther back and claims that
as early as the fourth century a process of "sabbathizing"
Sunday had started, which in his opinion is characterized
by a naturalistic idea of worship, by legalism and individu-
alism. These attitudes, which can still be found today, he
says, are opposed to any effort of renewal (the direction of
which one can guess to a certain extent from such hints).[12]
Here the Middle Ages have become gloomy again, and the
modern era again has become the real brightness that can
penetrate into the Church only with difficulty.

II. The Fundamental Theological Decision

Let us not proceed further here with the question of who
is right in his historical judgments or what the relative proportions of error and insight are. Discussing it would di-

[11] L. Brandolini, in *La domenica oggi: problemi e proposte pastorali*, ed. Ri-
naldo Falsini, Nuova collana liturgica, second series, 9 (Milan, Ed. O.R.,
1991), 378–95, citation at 380a.
[12] Ibid., 385f.

gress too far from our topic. In order to get to the bottom of the matter itself, let us try first to investigate in even greater depth the structure of Guardini's fundamental theological and intellectual decisions. Why, more particularly, is this step beyond the modern era important, what is its aim, and what reasons does it give to justify itself? I will try to elucidate this at first with two scenes from the autobiographical sketches; now that they are accessible to us, they have become a first-rate source of intellectual history. Guardini decided to continue in Tübingen in the autumn of 1906 the theological studies that he had begun in Freiburg; in doing so, he walked right into the middle of the drama of the Modernist crisis. On July 3, 1907, the Holy Office published the decree *Lamentabili*, which condemned the errors of the Modernists. On September 8 of the same year, the encyclical *Pascendi dominici gregis* appeared, which systematically justified the condemnations and attempted to describe a sort of modernistic systematic context that was seen behind the individual theses with which the debate of those days was directly concerned. The two documents had the effect of a declaration of war against everything that seemed modern and progressive in theology. No one who had anything to do with teaching or learning theology in Germany at that hour could remain unmoved by this challenge. Now granted, the faculty at Tübingen at that time was by no means as brilliant and avant-garde as one might imagine today. But since 1905, the chair for dogmatics had been occupied by Wilhelm Koch, a still very young but remarkable man, whom Guardini characterizes in a few telling strokes. Max Seckler has presented the facts about Wilhelm Koch in detail in a carefully balanced essay.[13] It is that much more moving now to be able to look at the events of that time

[13] M. Seckler, *Theologie vor Gericht: Der Fall Wilhelm Koch—Ein Bericht* (Tübingen, 1972).

through the eyes of someone who was there personally and was forced to find in them the fundamental decisions for his own path in life. Guardini summarized his judgment on Koch as follows: "His best virtues were honesty and conscientiousness. He was not a great theologian; for that he lacked an insight into what was essential and the power of synthesis; but he took truth seriously; you could sense that; in him it became part of his character."[14] From these sketches we see how much this man meant to Guardini: he owed him his liberation from the scrupulosity that had accompanied him from childhood on and increasingly threatened to become unbearable. It is exciting to see in Guardini's brief retrospect how a younger generation was finding its way, right there amid the climax of a crisis, and in doing so allowed itself neither to be compelled by external confidence in authority nor to be hindered by the pressures of human loyalties but, rather, discovered its decisions as a result of a new, interior contact with Christianity. Guardini remained grateful to Koch (who did not die until 1955) for the rest of his life and publicly expressed his gratitude in 1935 by dedicating his book on Pascal to his former teacher, when Koch had long since lost his position at the university. Yet already as a student he had broken with his thinking. Not as though Koch had actually taught anything heretical or had been a Modernist in the strict sense of the word. But the fundamental approach of his thought was for Guardini unsatisfactory. For if one worked as exclusively from historical documents and only with the historical-positivist method as Koch did, then adherence to dogma, which Koch no doubt wanted also, became laborious drudgery. It was then really nothing but a restriction of thought, a fetter faithfully endured, but not a source, not something that fructifies and

---

[14] R. Guardini, *Berichte über mein Leben* (Düsseldorf, 1984), 83.

widens horizons. Thus Guardini was able to able to appreciate Koch's thought, which he compared to "clean air and
clear space", but he felt just as plainly that it was "in and of
itself . . . simply too little".[15] He took along with him as
a gift lasting impressions of his professor's honesty, openness, and meticulousness, which would protect him against
all fanaticism and external dependence on authority, but he
was looking for a new foundation.

More precisely: he had already found it in the experience
of his conversion. In the short scene showing how he along
with his friend Karl Neundörfer—and yet each one individually—broke through to the faith again after having lost
it, there is something thrilling and inherently great precisely
because of the timidity and simplicity with which Guardini
describes the process. This experience in the attic and on
the balcony of Guardini's parents' house has an almost amaz-
ing resemblance to the scene in the garden in which Augustine and Alypius found the breakthrough of their lives. Both
times the innermost part of a man opens up, but in looking
into this utterly personal and intimate part, in listening to
a man's heartbeat, one hears all at once a major historical
hour striking, because it is an hour of truth, because a man
has been hit by the truth. Guardini had been moved by the
verse: "He who finds his life will lose it, and he who loses
his life will find it" (Mt 10:39). His soul had been penetrated by the intuition that this salvific giving could refer
only to God himself. But it had likewise become clear to
him that this could not mean God in general, intangibly and,
so, ultimately only a reflection of our own will, but rather
God concretely, as he stands before us in history. "There
must be, therefore, an objective authority that can draw my

---

[15] Ibid., 85.

response out of that hiding place of self-assertion. But there is only one: the Catholic Church in her authority and precision. The question of keeping or giving away one's soul is ultimately decided, not in the presence of God, but in the presence of the Church."[16] At that moment Guardini knew that he held everything—his whole life—in his hands, that he now had it at his disposal and had to dispose of it, and he gave his soul to the Church.[17] What happened to him in that moment he later described as the hope of a new approaching era: the Church had awakened in his soul. This moment was, at the same time, for him and his friend Neundörfer a farewell to Kant and neo-Kantianism, which had made such a forceful impression on them that their faith had crumbled. It was a farewell to what they had experienced as the modern era, *their* "end of the modern era", and their departure for new shores.

What at that time had been experience and practical knowledge now began, in the crisis surrounding Wilhelm Koch, to take on methodical shape for the path of his theological thought. As a result of that origin, it was clear to Guardini that independent, constructive theological knowledge could not come into being when Church and dogma appeared to be nothing but "limit and restriction".[18] He comes to the same problem again, moreover, in connection with his encounter with Franz Tillmann, a moral theologian in Bonn,

[16] Ibid., 72; cf. also Gerl, *Romano Guardini*, 42–44, which traces the subsequent influence of Matthew 10:39 on Guardini's work.

[17] Ibid., 72: "Then it seemed to me as though I were carrying everything—really, 'everything', my existence—in my hands, as though on a scale that was evenly balanced: 'I can make it tip to the right or to the left. I can give my soul away, or keep it. . . .' And then I tipped the scale to the right."

[18] Ibid., 85.

which at the beginning was so hopeful but then ended in disappointment. Once again he criticizes every sort of critical attitude, which for him basically was only "a kind of liberalism limited by obedience to dogma"[19]—and, thus, half-heartedness, from which nothing great can come, for in that way one is not truly liberal, nor can dogma become a meaningful factor in one's life and thinking. In opposition to this, Guardini sets his profession: "We were decidedly non-liberal."[20] This means that he and his friend were looking for a way in which revelation set its own standard and stood as the "decisive fact" of theological knowledge, with "the Church as its conveyor and dogma as the ordering of theological thought".[21] Then in the early 1920s, when Guardini appeared on the theological scene, he unexpectedly

[19] Ibid., 33.

[20] Ibid., 86.

[21] Ibid., 86. Guardini described this program at length in his lecture in Bonn "Anselm of Canterbury and the Nature of Theology", which has new relevance today and ought to be pondered deeply as a question put to contemporary theology. I will cite only a few characteristic sentences from it: "The Church alone knows God, insofar as something finite can know the Infinite. . . . What at first glance appeared to be the violation of all scientific thought is on deeper inspection the only possible foundation for theological science: The authentic subject of theology is the intellectual community of the Church" (*Auf dem Wege*, 58). "Someone is a theologian in the measure in which his epistemological attitude is extended and ordered to the historical and contemporary totality of the Church" (ibid., 59). His diaries show that Guardini remained entirely true to this position to the end. I refer simply to the entry dated September 28, 1954, about the Marian dogma of 1950, where he writes, among other things, "For one thing, it (= the dogma) makes it quite clear that the conveyor and norm of the content of the faith is not Scripture but rather the Church. And Scripture in the hands of the Church. I never thought otherwise. The Church is a prophet. She teaches and vouches. One must trust her. Anything else is half-measures and puts one in a false position." Hence it is a complete reversal of Guardini's position when

found himself in a climate in which the leading thinkers of the time were generally turning away from liberal theology, with Barth and Bultmann in the forefront; the correspondence between Erik Peterson and Adolf von Harnack about the Church and also Barth's debate with Harnack about the historical Jesus mark the new beginning, that seemed to be opening up on several sides.[22]

But we must not discuss that here, especially since Guardini himself seems to have cared little about those fellow travelers. We are concerned with the question about the foundations of his theological thought and their reliability, above and beyond the fascination exerted by his message in his historical hour. The real foundation of his theology—as I intended to show with these biographical flashbacks—was the experience of conversion that became for him simultaneously a way of overcoming the mentality of the modern era represented by Kant. In the beginning, there is not reflection but experience. Everything that appears later as content is developed from this original experience. I would like to try to list briefly, from this perspective, the main categories that became the basic framework for Guardini's thought.

Messerschmid says (and K. Rahner similarly) that due to the shock of the Modernist crisis he "remained within the limits that were set at that time". The opposite is true: Guardini was convinced that only thinking together with the subject Church makes one free and makes theology possible in the first place. Cf. Gerl, *Romano Guardini*, 57f.

[22] E. Peterson, *Theologische Traktate* (Munich, 1951); on pp. 293–321 is reprinted the correspondence with Harnack, which even today is still quite timely. On the dispute between Harnack and Barth and on the anti-liberal decision of the early Bultmann, cf. James McConkey Robinson, *A New Quest of the Historical Jesus* (London: SCM Press, 1959), 45ff.

III. Basic Categories of Guardini's Thought: The Unity of Liturgy, Christology, and Philosophical Understanding

1. *Thinking and being*

In the first place, we should mention the turn to the truth itself, the search for being behind doing. "Thought seems to want to turn reverently again to being"; so Guardini described this return to new metaphysical thinking in his trial lecture in Bonn, in which he cites in particular the work of Nikolai Hartmann.[23] The breakthrough out of Kant's perspective, which had been accomplished first in the work of Edmund Husserl, had meanwhile in fact broadened into a recommencement of metaphysical thinking; Max Scheler's conversion is to be understood in this context. If you read, for instance, the correspondence between Edith Stein and Hedwig Conrad-Martius, you can see how the sense of a great turning point was expressed in the phenomenological school and, thus, among the liveliest philosophical practitioners of the time: the optimism that philosophy, as an inquiry into things themselves, was now making a fresh start —a beginning that quite automatically pointed toward the great syntheses of the Middle Ages and the Catholic thought that was shaped by them.[24] It was a great hour for Catholicism, which for a moment attained a new historical luminosity.[25]

---

[23] *Auf dem Wege*, 45. On Guardini's relation to Scheler, see Gerl, *Romano Guardini*, 108–14 et passim.

[24] Unfortunately now I cannot find a copy of the little volume in which this correspondence was published by Kösel in the 1950s.

[25] Of course, the comment that Guardini added in 1923 to his 1920

It was from this perspective that Guardini conducted his debate with the Free German Youth and the Hohe Meißner formula, a kind of manifesto that articulated a program of self-determination, personal responsibility, and inner sincerity for the new youth movement. Guardini adopted these values in order to purify and deepen them at the same time: freedom—yes, but the only free person is someone "who is fully what he should be according to his nature". Hence, Guardini could coin the phrase, "Freedom is truth."[26] The truth of man is authenticity, conformity to one's nature, and now Guardini advanced straight to the heart of the Christian image of man: "But what is adoration? The obedience of being! . . . Thus, adoration is the primary obedience that serves as the foundation for all the rest: the obedience of our being to the being of God. If a being is in truth, then it itself is nothing but truth."[27] In such thought, liturgy is by no means aesthetic play or a sort of communal self-affirmation or pragmatic indoctrination. It is a summons of one's nature,

---

essay, "Vom Sinn des Gehorchens" [On the meaning of obedience] is indicative: he had replaced the expression "the Catholic man" with the formula "the man of the awakening era" and noted: "In 1920, the expression 'the Catholic man' still stood here. When this essay was written, one could still pronounce that expression without repugnance. There was a time—so short!—when it expressed jubilant discovery, a return to self of what is deepest within us. Now the lack of respect in speaking and writing has seized on it and made it vulgar. Now when cooler, critical heads take offense at it, they are right. Now! Who knows a way of protecting the sacredness of the word? We will have to stifle our favorite words!" In any case, this observation did not keep Guardini, a few lines earlier, from leaving the following sentence unaltered: "Catholic freedom—do you sense what that is? I do not know whether I have succeeded in saying what appears radiantly before my soul" (*Auf dem Wege*, 30).

[26] *Auf dem Wege*, 20.
[27] Ibid., 21.

a way to truth, because it corresponds to being. The fact that Guardini saw therein an affinity between his time and the Middle Ages is basically secondary. The decisive thing is that he emphasized openness to being as the potentiality and challenge of our existence. The decisive thing is that truth was a fundamental category of his thought and that, from that perspective, adoration and thought belonged together. This orientation was decisive for Guardini in the plan of his whole work, as his biographical account reveals even more insightfully than his early writings had done. He explains in these terms his conflict with Carl Sonnenschein. In contrast to the comment by that great pastoral worker, "We are in a beleaguered city; there are no problems in it, only slogans", he voiced his conviction: "Genuine praxis, however, in other words, right action, proceeds from the truth, and we must strive for this."[28] He returns to this idea repeatedly in his memoirs; I will mention only the sentence with which he concludes the account of his lectures in the Church of Saint Peter Canisius in Berlin: "Here I experienced most intensely what I said earlier about the power of truth. I have seldom been so conscious of how great, how fundamentally true and vital the Christian-Catholic message is as I was on those evenings. Sometimes it was as if Truth stood like a being in the room."[29] I think we will have to ponder in a completely new way these experiences and reflections of Guardini in the current debate over praxis as the standard of theology. The emphasis he placed on the priority of *logos* over *ethos* already in his first publication, in the splendid little volume entitled *The Spirit of the Liturgy*, was for him by no means a debate about theories but,

[28] *Berichte über mein Leben*, 111.
[29] Ibid., 114f., cf. 110.

rather, as practical as unpremeditated truth is practical just now.[30]

Moreover, this helps us to understand what separated him from the Maria Laach understanding of the liturgical movement and also from Klosterneuburg. The fact that [the Benedictine abbey of] Maria Laach was exclusively oriented toward the early Church and regarded the Middle Ages as a time of liturgical decline, whereas Guardini very deliberately referred to the Middle Ages and its metaphysical thought, may appear at first to be a superficial detail. The implications, however, run very deep. For it shows that their spiritual and intellectual foundations were not the same. Whereas for Guardini, adoration is derived from the claim of being, which then points to what is living and concrete, to the communitarian subject Church, Odo Casel rejected philosophical thought and philosophical logic as being foreign to mystery and wanted to seek only the form (the *eidos*) of the *mysterion*, which bears within itself its own logic, which cannot be deciphered philosophically. This resulted in a certain narrowness that had no sense of extra-liturgical piety and bore within itself a tendency to archaeological investigation aimed at a pristine restoration of an earlier age. Guardini's reference to the Middle Ages is of an entirely different sort. It is not a search for a bygone era but, rather, a longing for a new breakthrough to Being itself, the search for what is essential, which is found in the truth and not in a past form.[31]

---

[30] *The Spirit of the Liturgy*, 85–95; cf. J. Pieper, *Noch wußte es niemand: Autobiographische Aufzeichnungen 1904–1945* (Munich, 1976), 70.

[31] On Guardini's conflict with Maria Laach, cf. Gerl, *Romano Guardini*, 127–30.

2. *Antithesis and concrete existence: From liturgy to Christology and popular piety*

Together with the category of obedience to being, we have already discovered now a set of further categories: essentiality, which Guardini contrasted to a merely subjective truthfulness; the obedience that follows from man's relation to the truth and expresses his way of becoming free, of being at one with his nature; adoration as the core of the perception and acceptance of truth; finally, the priority of *logos* over *ethos*, of being over doing. Now we must investigate two more basic categories, which again are closely related: concrete existence and the antithesis. As early as 1917, Guardini had presented a sort of outline of his philosophical intuition under the title "Antithesis and Antitheses: Sketches of a Systematic Doctrine of Types"; in 1925, the work assumed its definitive form under the title *Der Gegensatz: Versuche zu einer Philosophie des Lebendig-Konkreten* [Antithesis: Essays on a philosophy of concrete existence].[32] Instead of theoretical considerations, I would like to attempt to illustrate what concerns me here by means of a text by Guardini that at the same time leads us directly from liturgy into Christology and into the context of both. I mean the "Dialogue about the Riches of Christ", published in 1923, the idea for which came to Guardini during a nocturnal hike from Bonn to Holtorf, as he described in his memoirs.[33] It seems to me that in this short and exceedingly lively essay, the weave of Guardini's thought becomes clearer than almost anywhere else. Three persons are conversing: the secretary of *Cari-*

---

[32] The treatment of the theme of antithesis is one of the main ideas of the Guardini biography by H.-B. Gerl, to which I must refer again on this question.

[33] *Berichte über mein Leben*, 35.

tas, the scholar, and the assistant pastor, in whom the inner antitheses of Guardini's own thought clash, while in the background appears the half-rationalistic friend Windecker, whom Guardini may have modeled on men whom he respected, such as Wilhelm Koch or Fritz Tillmann, who remained present in his thought as a corrective and query, without having become a part of his own inner struggle, so to speak. Nevertheless, the exchange among the three who are there together (each of whom is Guardini himself) is tense and contradictory enough. They are three methods of Christology in debate with one another—not just ways of thinking, but, rather, fundamental attitudes, forms of piety and of Christian life. The secretary of *Caritas* has just come home from devotions to the Sacred Heart and is quite angry that he found so much kitsch and artificiality in them. He is a man of sound, robust piety that is nourished entirely on the Jesus of the synoptic Gospels, on the austere figure of Jesus as Mark especially depicts him. In this Jesus, the divine is "so reserved, so chaste, I might say. It hides itself. . . . The divine in him is like religion in a chaste soul. It blushes when it speaks about its God. . . ."[34] When the rich young man addresses him as "good Master", Jesus refuses it as something sentimental and inappropriate. Jesus does not want this man with his religious longing to stop at him or to try to make him the endpoint of his religious impulse. And now, in the Sacred Heart devotions, one hears on all sides again and again, "Heart of Jesus, sweetest Heart of Jesus" . . . "and with the singing and the picture up front and everything, I ran out. Tell me, now, is that Jesus? Is that his Spirit?"[35]

The scholar and the secretary of *Caritas* are quite in agreement in their discomfort with the Sacred Heart devotions.

[34] *Auf dem Wege*, 158.
[35] Ibid., 152.

Only their reasons for it are different, and therefore so are their positive decisions. What bothers the scholar about the Sacred Heart devotions is their lack of culture, which, he suspects, conceals an intrinsic hostility to culture.[36] "For what dominates in the Sacred Heart devotions is not the Logos but, rather, the will, love, the *alogon* (Word-lessness), and, consequently, the whole force of subjectivity." That is why the scholar waxes enthusiastic about the liturgy, in which "everything is subdued, illuminated". "The Logos lives in it. All the fervor has become light, and all the gushing has become form." In all this he finds a wonderful affirmation of reality. "Above all, certainly, there is the sacrifice, but it seems to be there only so as to make the affirmation purer and freer: the supernatural itself becomes quite 'natural' . . . the antithesis of everything we call artificial."[37] Consequently, what really bothers him about the Sacred Heart devotions is not the lack of the historical, living character of Jesus but, rather, their artificiality. "In the liturgy, too, it is not so much Jesus of Nazareth . . . , but, rather, 'the Word-made-flesh', the God-man. But that is an accretion resulting from the full affirmation. The image of Jesus in the liturgy . . . is to the historical Jesus . . . as the pure circle of mathematics is to the circle drawn with chalk."[38] Now the secretary of *Caritas* can no longer agree with that. Actually, he has nothing against the irrational aspect of the Sacred Heart devotions. He feels repelled by the schematic quality, the disappearance of the details, of the irreplaceable fragrance that the figure of Jesus has in the Gospels, of the tone and color, of the expressive line and the fresh, living quality. "Jesus of Nazareth, before whom men bow and listen with hungry hearts to the sound of his voice, becomes

[36] Ibid., 153.
[37] Ibid., 155.
[38] Ibid., 154f.

'the Heart'! An 'it', a neuter noun, a thing!" "That is why I do not like the liturgy, either. . . . In it I do not recognize the Lord. That is not Jesus of Nazareth at all."[39] In contrast to the chaste reserve of the Gospels, the liturgy transfigures everything. "That may be good for heaven, but here on earth. . . ." The secretary of *Caritas* is attentive enough to add that in this sense the Gospel of John and the Book of Revelation are already "liturgy", too.[40]

At this point, the speech for the defense by the assistant pastor begins, who in his encounters with simple people has learned what forces the Sacred Heart devotions can release. He does not dispute the lack of culture in this type of piety. But he reminds the others that Christ did not save the world through reason and culture but, rather, through a criminal's death on a gibbet. "What works and builds up . . . are the sufferings of the persecuted, the sacrifices of the forgotten, the works of the despised. . . . And when nothing else can help any more, no advice and no culture and no clever book, then what still helps is suffering offered to God in secret."[41] At this point, Guardini, who often had to defend himself against the accusation of aestheticism and academism, adopts a passionate, almost revolutionary tone. The assistant pastor recalls the Russian Revolution, in which burst forth primordial forces that could not be dismissed as mere stupidity and criminality. Here passionate feeling was seeking the way to man and was sacrificing everything for it. "For this cause, it also destroyed everything, all the beautiful, well-balanced culture. . . . And yet it will perish, because it is only nature and fallen nature." But the Christian response could only be a primordial will that comes from those same depths. "It could only be a sentiment that is pure love. . . . Failure is

[39] Ibid., 158.
[40] Ibid., 158f.
[41] Ibid., 161.

its most powerful force, . . . and external recognition and success are the signs that it has missed the right path. . . . The end times have started! Do you think that history and culture will still be any help then? Only one thing is left now: the hatred of the Antichrist and, resisting him, the soul that has unconditionally placed itself at God's disposal, the soul that is only one thing and wants only one thing: love."[42] The secretary of *Caritas* replies, "Yes, you have seen Christ."[43] In the "blessed hour" of this conversation, concrete existence opens up, and the connection between *logos* and *alogon* is part of it. Finally it is the secretary of *Caritas* who, after an initial attempt by the scholar, puts the insight of the hour into words: "Every feature of the Gospel reality is infinitely precious, but we see it correctly only in light of the essential truth as it speaks to us out of eternity into our present day through the Church."[44]

In this seemingly very simple sentence, Guardini's christological synthesis, his theology of the liturgy, and his philosophical conception are reduced to a concise formula; Guardini's gift was the ability to say great things simply. Man is open to the truth, but the truth is not out there somewhere; rather, it is in concrete existence, in the figure of Jesus Christ. This concrete existence proves to be the truth precisely by the fact that it is the union of what is seemingly antithetical: *logos* and *alogon* are united in it. Truth exists only in the whole. And the whole is found only where antitheses are bridged. Once again, the consequence of this for Guardini's view of the liturgy is that, contrary to the interpretations advocated in Maria Laach, he affirmed develop-

[42] Ibid., 163. Precisely in these sentences we may hear an echo of Guardini's conversion experience.

[43] Ibid., 164.

[44] Ibid., 165.

ment and, thus, the modern era also, with its subjectivism, as part concrete existence and its antitheses. From this logically followed his approval of popular piety and rejection of all liturgical exclusivity. For Christology, this means that no adequate image of Christ can be based on the selection, reduction, separation, or elimination of sources. Thought that compels one to resort to those measures is ultimately not sufficiently critical. It makes itself into the standard. Our thinking is not the beginning that sets the standards; rather, he is, who shatters all standards and cannot be grasped in any unity that we might devise. He himself is the beginning and proves himself to be the beginning precisely by the fact that we cannot manage to fit him into a consistent type and explain him psychologically. Anyone who wants to see Christ must "change his ways", must step out of the autonomy of his arbitrary thinking into a listening willingness to accept what is. Here the demand of phenomenological philosophy for the obedience of thought to being, obedience vis-à-vis what manifests itself and what is, fuses with the basic idea of faith, which is turning one's life around so that it *accepts* a new standard that is given and understands everything in a new way in terms of it.[45] Epistemology becomes training in faith. This synthesis of thought, which never gives up its philosophical seriousness and the breadth of its search for the whole but, rather, in the radicalness of this inquiry eventually goes beyond all mere theorizing, appears movingly at the beginning of the little book in the sentences about the image of Jesus the Christ in the New Testament, which express the inner orientation of all Guardini's christological statements: Perhaps in our search for the image of Jesus we will:

[45] *Das Bild von Jesus dem Christus nach dem Neuen Testament* (Freiburg: Herderbücherei, 1962), 139f.

not even arrive at a "figure" but only at a series of lines
that soar beyond our field of vision. Perhaps we will learn
that the Ascension means, not just a one-time event in the
life of Jesus, but generally the way in which he is given
to us: as he disappears into heaven, into what is reserved
by God. But even then these lines are precious: they are
signposts to the transcendent step of faith, and the fact
that they are taken from our sight is the reason for that
failure that teaches us to adore.[46]

IV. Epilogue: Guardini and
the German University

Given his way of thinking, Guardini had a hard time along
the way to an academic teaching position. Around the turn
of the century, scholarship, for which the university exists,
was either natural science or historiography. And so theology, in order to remain worthy of being a university subject,
retreated into historiography. "To do scholarly theological
work meant to determine what one era and the next, or this
man and that man, had thought about a question. . . . But
what interested me spontaneously was not the question of
what someone said about Christian truth, but rather what
is true."[47] Even when he held a teaching position in Berlin,
Guardini still suffered from the fact that he seemed to be
beyond the methodological pale of the university, by which
he was in fact publicly rejected.[48] He consoled himself with
the idea that with his struggle to be understood, with his
judgments and character, he could be a forerunner of a kind

[46] Ibid., 28.
[47] *Berichte über mein Leben*, 24.
[48] Ibid., 41.

of university that did not yet exist.[49] It is to the credit of the
German university that even with his idiosyncratic way he
was able to find a place in it and was increasingly able to experience it as the home of his special vocation. Thus after the
[Second World] War, in a major academic speech about the
Jewish question, Romano Guardini passionately defended
the university as the place where the truth is sought; as the
place where men are measured by the standards of the great
past; as the place of the most vigilant responsibility for the
general public. He defended the German university, also,
because during the Third Reich he had experienced its collapse, which followed by an inner logic from its retreat into
an apparent lack of presuppositions and from the repression
of the question of truth by the prevailing academic method.
As a result of this experience, and of his knowledge about
what a university can and must be, he then took a stance
with a passionate entreaty, which otherwise seemed quite
unlike him, against the politicization of the university and its
infiltration by a partisan administration, the jargon of meetings, and the tumult of the street, and exhorted his listeners:
"Ladies and gentlemen: Do not allow that! This concerns
something that affects what is common to all of us, future
history."[50] Once again: it is to the credit of the German university that Romano Guardini was able to find his place in
it and regarded it as his home. Thus, after the humiliations
of National Socialism, it was rehabilitated as an open forum
of that great and earnest search for truth. But the figure of
Guardini, his way of thinking, remains a question put to
the university; today one must call out again and louder to
the students: Do not let political passion suffocate the free

[49] Ibid., 46.
[50] *Verantwortung: Gedanken zur jüdischen Frage* (Munich, 1952), 41.

word of the search for truth. "Do not allow that!" Guardini remains a standard for our university, and we should all be concerned that it firmly upholds that standard today and tomorrow as well.

BIBLIOGRAPHICAL NOTES

Many of the speeches given by Joseph Ratzinger at the Catholic Academy in Bavaria were subsequently reprinted in various anthologies published in German and English:

1. "Der Primat des Papstes und die Einheit des Gottesvolkes", in *Dienst an der Einheit: Zum Wesen und Auftrag des Petrusamtes*, ed. J. Ratzinger (Düsseldorf, 1978), 165–79; reprinted in *Kirche, Ökumene und Politik* (Cinisello Balsamo, Italy: Edizioni Paoline, 1987); translated by Michael J. Miller as "The Primacy of the Pope and the Unity of the People of God", in *Church, Ecumenism, and Politics: New Endeavors in Ecclesiology* (San Francisco: Ignatius Press, 2008), 36–50.

2. "Das Problem der Absolutheit des christlichen Heilsweges", in W. Böld et al., *Kirche in der ausserchristlichen Welt* (Regensburg, 1967), 7–29; reprinted in *Das neue Volk Gottes: Entwürfe zur Ekklesiologie* (Düsseldorf, 1969); an earlier English translation appeared in *Teaching All Nations* 4 (1967): 183–97.

3. "Schwierigkeiten mit dem Apostolicum: Höllenfahrt—Himmelfahrt—Auferstehung des Fleisches" consists of excerpts from two chapters of *Einführung in das Christentum* (Munich: Kösel-Verlag, 1968); translated by J. R. Foster as *Introduction to Christianity* (London: Burns & Oates, 1969); English edition revised by Michael J.

Miller (San Francisco: Ignatius Press, 2004), 293–314, 347–56.

4. "Das Heil des Menschen—innerweltlich und christlich", not previously published.

5. "Wesen und Grenzen der Kirche", in *Das Zweite Vatikanische Konzil*, edited by K. Forster, Studien und Berichte der Katholischen Akademie in Bayern, vol. 24 (Würzburg: Echter-Verlag, 1963), 47–68. Reprinted in *Das neue Volk Gottes* (see note 2 above).

6. "Warum ich noch in der Kirche bin", in H.U. von Balthasar and J. Ratzinger, *Zwei Plädoyers* (Munich: Kösel, 1971), 55–75; translated by John Griffiths as "Why I Am Still in the Church", in *Two Say Why* (Chicago: Franciscan Herald Press, 1973); later translated by Michael J. Miller in *Credo for Today* (San Francisco: Ignatius Press, 2009), 181–200.

7. "Europa—Verpflichtendes Erbe für die Christen", in *Kirche, Ökumene und Politik* (see note 1); translated by Michael J. Miller as "Europe: A Heritage with Obligations for Christians", in *Church, Ecumenism, and Politics*, 209–22.

8. The first major section of the speech "Interpretation— Kontemplation—Aktion: Überlegungen zum Auftrag einer Katholischen Akademie" (found under the heading "I. Was konstituiert eine Akademie?") was reprinted as "Zum Wesen des Akademischen und seiner Freiheit", in *Wesen und Auftrag der Theologie* (Einsiedeln: Johannes Verlag, 1993), 26–36; translated by Adrian Walker as "On the Essence of the Academy and Its Freedom", in *The Nature and Mission of Theology* (San Francisco, Ignatius Press, 1995), 31–41.

9. "Vorpolitische moralische Grundlagen eines freiheitlichen Staates", in Jürgen Habermas and Joseph Ratzinger, *Dialektik der Säkularisierung: Über Vernunft und Religion* (Herder Verlag, 2005), translated by Brian McNeil as *The Dialectics of Secularization: On Reason and Religion* (San Francisco, Ignatius Press, 2006).

10. "Laudatio auf Ministerpräsident Dr. h. c. Alfons Goppel", not previously published.

11. "Von der Liturgie zur Christologie: Romano Guardinis theologischer Grundsatz und seine Aussagekraft", in J. Ratzinger, ed., *Wege zur Wahrheit: Die bleibende Bedeutung von Romano Guardini* (Düsseldorf, 1985); not previously published in English.